The Essentials of Edexcel GCSE Additional Science is matched to the **Edexcel GCSE in Additional Science specification (2103)**.

It provides full coverage of the three units: **Biology 2, Chemistry 2 and Physics 2**, and pages are **colour-coded** so that you can distinguish between them easily.

The content for each unit is divided into four **topics** to correspond with the specification and provide a clear, manageable structure to your revision.

At the end of each topic there is a **glossary of key words**. These pages can be used as checklists to help you with your revision. Make sure you are familiar with all the words listed and understand their meanings and relevance – they are central to your understanding of that topic!

As a revision guide, this book focuses on the material which is externally assessed (i.e. tested under exam conditions). It does not cover the practical skills assessment and assessment activities, which are marked by your teacher.

There are several assessment routes available. Depending on the assessment route you take, you will have to sit up to three **multiple-choice tests** and three **structured question papers**, which each count for 10% of your final mark (up to 60% in total). Each multiple-choice test and structured question paper covers one of the three units. The contents list in this revision guide clearly identifies the three separate units, so that you can prepare for each paper individually.

This guide can be used to revise for either the **Foundation** or **Higher Tier** papers.

> The material that is limited to Higher Tier is enclosed in a coloured box, and can be easily identified by the symbol **HT** *.

At the end of the book, you will find a detailed **periodic table** which will provide a useful reference when you are studying the chemistry unit.

Spellings within this guide may differ from the British standard. This is to ensure that spellings correspond with those on the specification and reflect those that will appear on your test papers.

Don't just read the information in this guide – **learn actively!** Jot down anything you think will help you to remember, no matter how trivial it may seem, and constantly test yourself without looking at the text.

Good luck with your exams!

Information About the Authors

Aleksander Jedrosz (Biology) is an experienced GCSE science teacher and examiner, currently working as a Curriculum Coordinator for the Sciences at a city academy. He is already the author of a book about the human eye.

Susan Loxley (Chemistry) has an excellent understanding of the applications of science in industry, having been involved in the development of materials for aerospace for 8 years. She now teaches chemistry to KS3 and KS4 pupils and is an examiner for GCSE science.

Dr Ron Holt (Physics) has over ten years' teaching experience within large comprehensive schools. He has worked as a research scientist of physics in a prestigious university and has been involved in a number of science publications.

*Higher Tier material correct at time of going to print.

GW00419776

Contents

Contents

Inside Living Cells

DNA and Chromosomes

In normal human cells there are 23 pairs of **chromosomes**. Chromosomes consist of long, coiled molecules of **DNA** (deoxyribonucleic acid).

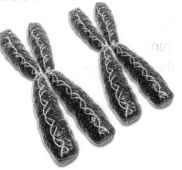

A gene is a section of DNA, which codes for a particular inherited characteristic, such as having attached or unattached earlobes.

A DNA molecule consists of two strands, which are coiled to form a **double helix**. The strands are linked by a series of paired **bases**: adenine (A), cytosine (C), guanine (G) and thymine (T).

- Adenine is only ever linked to thymine: A–T.
- Cytosine is only ever linked to guanine: C–G.

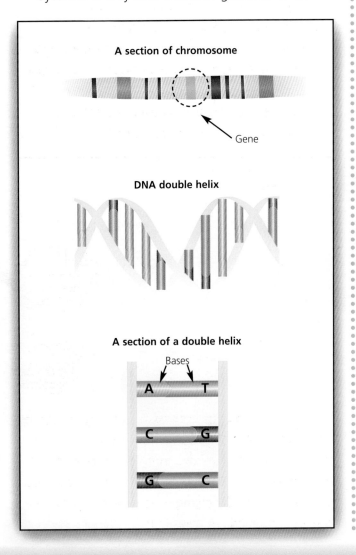

A section of chromosome

Gene

DNA double helix

A section of a double helix

Bases

A   T

C   G

G   C

How DNA Works

DNA contains the instructions for how the cells will join amino acids together in order to make specific proteins.

The instructions are in the form of a code, made up of the four bases (adenine, thymine, cytosine and guanine). The sequence of bases represents the order in which a cell should assemble amino acids to make a protein.

There are about 20 amino acids in total which can be arranged in different orders and combinations to produce different proteins.

Proteins are molecules that the body requires to make hormones, skin and hair etc., and for growth and repair.

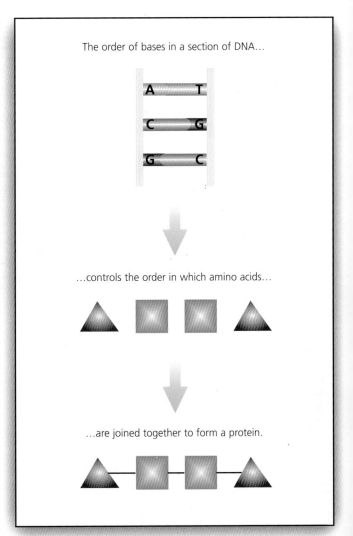

The order of bases in a section of DNA…

A   T

C   G

G   C

…controls the order in which amino acids…

…are joined together to form a protein.

Making Proteins

Organelles are specialised structures found in the cytoplasm of cells. Organelles called **ribosomes** are involved in **protein synthesis**.

The information needed to make a protein is stored in the DNA of a gene. The bases in DNA occur as **triplets** (e.g. ACG or ACC). Each triplet codes for a single amino acid in a protein. This code is stored in the **coding strand** of DNA and is copied to produce a molecule of RNA (ribonucleic acid). RNA is similar to DNA but, unlike DNA, it only has one strand and it can move outside the nucleus of the cell into the cytoplasm. The RNA contains the code for linking the amino acids; the ribosomes interpret this code to link the amino acids and form a **polypeptide** (protein).

DNA in nucleus of cell	→	RNA	→	Ribosomes	→	Polypeptide (protein) in cytoplasm

A Cell

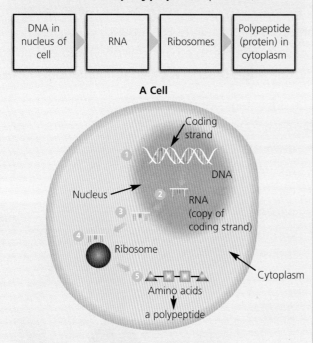

1. DNA unravels at the correct gene.
2. A copy of the coding strand is made to produce RNA.
3. The copy moves from the nucleus into the cytoplasm.
4. The triplet code is decoded by the ribosomes.
5. Amino acids join to each other in the correct order to form a polypeptide (protein).

Genetic Engineering

Sections of DNA that code for a specific protein can be transferred into **microorganisms**. The microorganisms then reproduce and make large quantities of the protein. This method can be used to produce lots of useful substances. For example, bacteria can be used to produce large quantities of the hormone **insulin** (a protein) for use by diabetics:

1. The gene for insulin production is identified. It is removed using a special enzyme, called a restriction enzyme, which cuts through the DNA strands in precise places.
2. Another restriction enzyme is used to cut open a ring of bacterial DNA (**a plasmid**). Other enzymes are then used to insert the section of human DNA into the plasmid.
3. The plasmid is inserted into a bacterium which starts to divide rapidly and, as it divides, it replicates the plasmid. The bacteria are cultivated on a large scale in **fermenters** and soon there are millions of bacteria, each carrying instructions to make insulin. When the bacteria then make the protein (insulin), commercial quantities of insulin are produced.

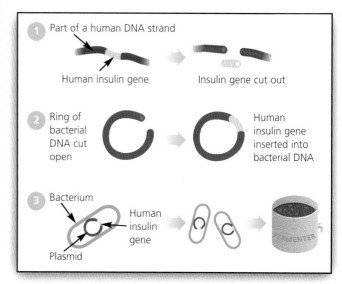

Fermentation is the process by which microorganisms take food from their environment, as an energy source, and excrete waste substances, like carbon dioxide, changing the substances in the surrounding medium over time.

Inside Living Cells

A fermenter is a controlled environment which provides ideal conditions for the microorganisms to live, feed and produce the proteins needed.

HT A fermenter is a large vessel used to cultivate microorganisms. It requires...

- **aseptic (sterile) conditions** – the microorganisms must not become contaminated by other microorganisms
- **nutrients** – the fermenter must contain the nutrients that the particular microorganisms need in order to grow
- **an optimum temperature** – suitable for the microorganisms to grow. (In schools, microorganisms are kept at a maximum of 25°C. In industry, higher temperatures can be used to produce more rapid growth.)
- **the correct pH level**
- **oxygenation** – microorganisms need oxygen to respire
- **agitation (stirring)** – to maintain an even temperature.

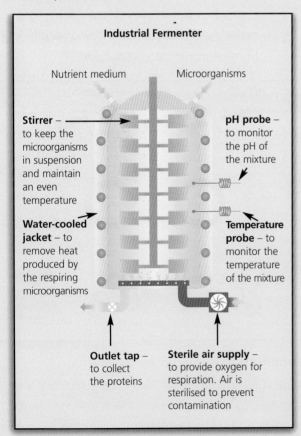

Industrial Fermenter

Nutrient medium   Microorganisms

Stirrer – to keep the microorganisms in suspension and maintain an even temperature

pH probe – to monitor the pH of the mixture

Water-cooled jacket – to remove heat produced by the respiring microorganisms

Temperature probe – to monitor the temperature of the mixture

Outlet tap – to collect the proteins

Sterile air supply – to provide oxygen for respiration. Air is sterilised to prevent contamination

Microorganisms and Food Production

Microorganisms can be used in some types of food production. The table below gives some examples.

	Microorganism	Sugar Supply	Result
Bread	Yeast	Sugar is added to flour	Released carbon dioxide makes bread rise
Beer	Yeast	Starch in barley is broken down into sugar (malting)	Alcohol – hops added to give flavour
Wine	Yeast	Grapes	Alcohol – flavour depends on grapes used
Yoghurt	Bacteria	Milk sugar (lactose)	Lactic acid clots milk and thickens it

Yeast is a single-celled microorganism. In the presence of oxygen it converts glucose to water and carbon dioxide. In the absence of oxygen it converts glucose to ethanol (alcohol) and carbon dioxide – this process is called fermentation.

The advantages of using microorganisms to produce food are that they...

- grow and reproduce quickly
- are easy to handle and manipulate
- can be produced indoors (they are not dependent on climate)
- can make use of waste products from other industrial processes.

Aerobic Respiration

Energy is produced by aerobic respiration. Blood transports oxygen and food, in the form of **glucose**, to the body's cells. Special enzymes in the cells cause the glucose and oxygen to react, and energy is released. The energy can then be used for work, e.g. movement. This process is called **aerobic respiration**.

Glucose, oxygen and carbon dioxide move between the capillaries and the respiring cells by **diffusion** (i.e. from high concentration to low concentration) down a concentration gradient: glucose and oxygen diffuse from the capillaries into respiring cells; carbon dioxide diffuses from respiring cells into the capillaries.

Aerobic respiration is a very efficient method of producing energy: one molecule of glucose respired aerobically can provide 20 times as much energy as anaerobic respiration (see p.8).

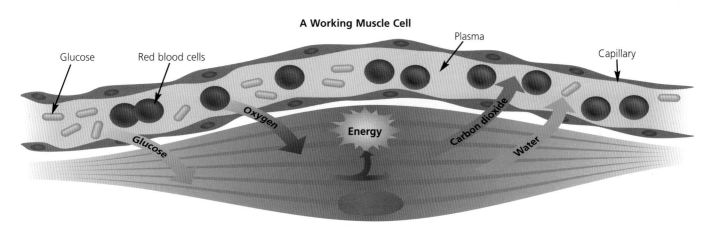

A Working Muscle Cell

The Equation

Glucose + Oxygen →	Carbon dioxide	+	Water	+	Energy
$C_6H_{12}O_6$ + $6O_2$ →	$6CO_2$	+	$6H_2O$	+	Joules
Glucose and **oxygen** are brought to the respiring cells by the bloodstream.	**Carbon dioxide** is taken away by the blood to the lungs, where it is breathed out.	**Water** passes into the blood and is lost as sweat, moist breath and urine.		**Energy** is used for muscle contraction, metabolism and maintaining temperature.

Increased Diffusion

When muscle cells are working hard (contracting and relaxing a lot), their respiration rates increase because more energy is being used up. This means that more oxygen needs to be absorbed and more carbon dioxide needs to be removed. This gas exchange takes place by diffusion in the lungs, at an increased rate.

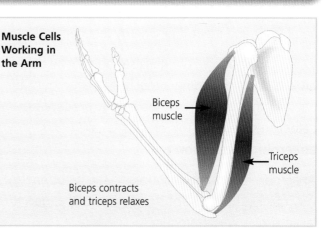

Muscle Cells Working in the Arm

Biceps muscle

Triceps muscle

Biceps contracts and triceps relaxes

Inside Living Cells

The Effects of Exercise

When you exercise (i.e. when you increase your physical activity), your breathing rate increases so that large quantities of oxygen can enter the body and larger quantities of carbon dioxide can be removed. As both of these gases are being transported by the blood, the heart rate has to increase.

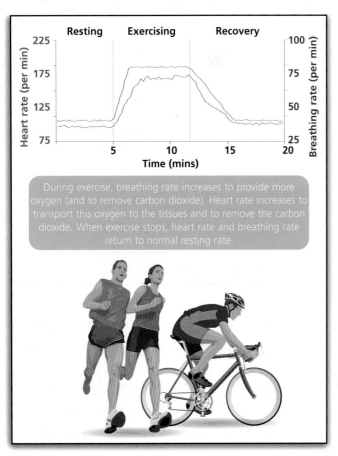

During exercise, breathing rate increases to provide more oxygen (and to remove carbon dioxide). Heart rate increases to transport this oxygen to the tissues and to remove the carbon dioxide. When exercise stops, heart rate and breathing rate return to normal resting rate.

Anaerobic Respiration

During vigorous exercise, the lungs and the bloodstream cannot always deliver enough oxygen to the muscle cells to respire the available glucose aerobically and meet their energy requirements.

When this happens, the glucose can only be partly broken down, releasing a much smaller amount of energy (only about $\frac{1}{20}$ of the energy produced by aerobic respiration). This process is called **anaerobic respiration**.

Anaerobic respiration produces a little bit of energy very quickly, but most of the glucose is changed to lactic acid, a waste product.

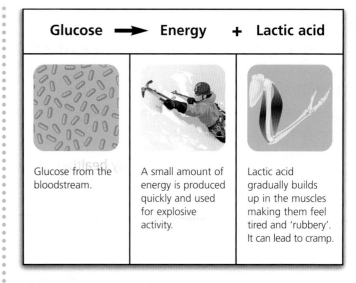

Glucose ➡ Energy + Lactic acid

| Glucose from the bloodstream. | A small amount of energy is produced quickly and used for explosive activity. | Lactic acid gradually builds up in the muscles making them feel tired and 'rubbery'. It can lead to cramp. |

Oxygen Debt

The build up of lactic acid causes acute fatigue in the muscles and results in an '**oxygen debt**'. This causes the muscles to stop contracting efficiently.

After exercise, the lactic acid must be broken down quickly to avoid cell damage; the oxygen debt must be 'repaid' through deep breathing. This provides enough oxygen to oxidise the lactic acid into carbon dioxide and water.

Monitoring Changes

Medical staff often need to monitor a patient's temperature, breathing rate and heart rate. This used to be done manually, by observing the patient and checking their pulse rate at frequent intervals.

However, all this can now be done using digital thermometers and electronic breathing-rate and heart-rate monitors. This means that...
- more reliable data can be collected – it is free from human error
- monitors can be left on constantly – this provides a more accurate overall picture of a patient's health.

Technological advances mean that this type of equipment is now cheaper to produce, so it is also used by sports scientists and in gyms.

Diet and Exercise

In today's society we are constantly bombarded with advice about what to eat and how much exercise we should take in order to maintain a healthy lifestyle.

Obesity is very common in the UK, especially in young people, and the number of cases is increasing. So what can we do to stay healthy?

Diet

It is important to eat a **balanced diet**, i.e. a diet which includes all the basic food groups in the correct proportions. A balanced diet provides the body with the energy and nutrients it needs to work properly. This is especially important for children and teenagers, who are still growing and developing.

The amount of energy needed depends on the individual. For example, a person who carries out manual work will need more energy than someone who works in an office. If you take in more energy (through food and drink) than you use (for growth, movement etc.), you will put on weight.

Recommended Portions per Day

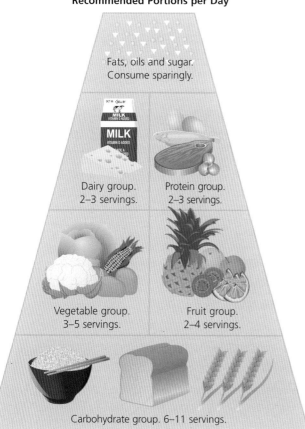

Fats, oils and sugar. Consume sparingly.

Dairy group. 2–3 servings.

Protein group. 2–3 servings.

Vegetable group. 3–5 servings.

Fruit group. 2–4 servings.

Carbohydrate group. 6–11 servings.

Exercise

Exercise is important in order to keep healthy. You should exercise for about 20 minutes, four or five times a week, and aim to increase your heart rate by approximately 75%. Most people have a resting heart rate of 70–75 beats per minute (bpm). Activities like football and tennis will increase your heart rate to about 120bpm.

Official advice about diet and exercise has changed over time because…

- our lifestyles have changed (for example, cars and machines mean that we walk less and carry out less manual work)
- our understanding of how the human body works has developed, meaning we know more about the effects of eating certain foods, not doing enough exercise etc.
- new scientific research can change how we feel about different foods (for example, when research suggests health risks that could be associated with certain foods).

'Fashionable' Diets

Some 'fashionable' diets do have a scientific basis. For example, a low-carbohydrate diet leads to weight loss because carbohydrates are our main source of energy. Without carbohydrates, the body has to start breaking down essential fat and protein stores to release glucose for respiration. However, diets like this, over long periods of time, are not healthy because they are not balanced.

Inside Living Cells

Glossary

Adenine – one of four bases found in DNA; it pairs up with thymine and is part of the basis of the genetic code

Aerobic – in the presence of oxygen. Aerobic respiration uses oxygen to release energy and produce carbon dioxide and water

Amino acid – a molecule containing carbon, oxygen, hydrogen, nitrogen and (often) sulphur. Amino acids link up to make proteins

Anaerobic – in the absence of oxygen. Anaerobic respiration is the incomplete breakdown of glucose to release a small amount of energy

Bases – the four basic units of the genetic code (adenine, thymine, cytosine and guanine)

Capillary – the smallest of the body's blood vessels. Their walls are only one cell thick and they have a very small internal diameter – red blood cells have to squeeze through in single file

Coding – instructions for assembling amino acids to build proteins

Cramp – muscular pain caused when muscles are overworked and lactic acid builds up. Muscles cannot contract any more until lactic acid is removed

Cultivated – growing and nurturing an organism (often to produce or enhance a particular feature)

Cytosine – one of four bases found in DNA; it pairs up with guanine and is part of the basis of the genetic code

Diffusion – the movement of a substance from a region of high concentration to a region of low concentration down a concentration gradient

DNA (deoxyribonucleic acid) – the material found in chromosomes. It is a double-stranded molecule that is held together by four bases (adenine, thymine, cytosine and guanine), which form the genetic code

Double helix – the shape of a DNA molecule – two twisted strands linked by the bases

Fermentation – the process by which microorganisms obtain energy from a medium and produce other substances through respiration,

changing the chemical composition of the medium. When yeast does this, glucose is converted to carbon dioxide and alcohol

Glucose – a simple sugar or carbohydrate; reacts with oxygen in the body to release energy

Guanine – one of four bases found in DNA; it pairs up with cytosine and is part of the basis of the genetic code

Insulin – a hormone produced by the pancreas which controls blood sugar levels

Lactic acid – produced by animal cells during the incomplete breakdown of glucose during anaerobic respiration

Microorganism – a living organism that is so small a microscope is needed to see it

Protein – a food group that contains carbon, hydrogen, oxygen, nitrogen and (often) sulphur. Proteins are made up of long chains of amino acids

Respiration – the process by which energy is released from glucose

Strand – refers to a single strand of the double-stranded DNA; the closely related RNA molecule only has a single strand

Thymine – one of four bases found in DNA; it pairs up with adenine and is part of the basis of the genetic code

---

Aseptic – sterile; free from contamination

Organelle – any structure that is found inside a cell and that has a particular job to perform, e.g. the nucleus, mitochondria and ribosomes

Polypeptide – a single-chain molecule of many amino acids joined together by peptide bonds. Protein is a polypeptide

Ribosome – a cell organelle involved in protein synthesis

RNA (ribonucleic acid) – a single-stranded molecule (which contains the bases adenine, uracil, cytosine and guanine). It is involved in protein synthesis

Triplet – a sequence of three bases in a gene that codes for a single amino acid

Mitosis

Mitosis is the division of a cell nucleus to produce two cell nuclei with **genetically identical** sets of chromosomes. This happens in order to produce new cells for growth and for the replacement of tissues. The diagram opposite shows this process:

1. Cell with two pairs of chromosomes.
2. Each chromosome replicates itself.
3. The copies separate. Cell now divides.
4. Each new cell has the same number of chromosomes as the original cell and contains the same genes as the original cell.

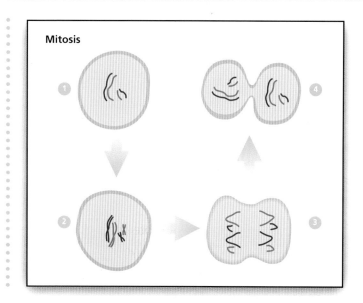

Mitosis

Meiosis

In **meiosis**, a **diploid nucleus** divides twice to produce four **haploid** nuclei which contain half the number of chromosomes. A diploid nucleus contains two sets of chromosomes. A haploid nucleus contains only one set of chromosomes.

This process produces cells with **genetically different** sets of chromosomes and happens in sexually reproducing organisms to produce **gametes** (sex cells, i.e. sperm and ova).

	Mitosis	Meiosis
Where it happens	In most parts of the body.	In the ovaries and testes.
Number of cells made	Two cells.	Four cells.
Genetic variation	All cells are genetically identical.	All cells are genetically different.
Number of chromosomes in the nucleus	Two sets of chromosomes – diploid.	One set of chromosomes – haploid.
Purpose	Growth and cell replacement.	Production of gametes.

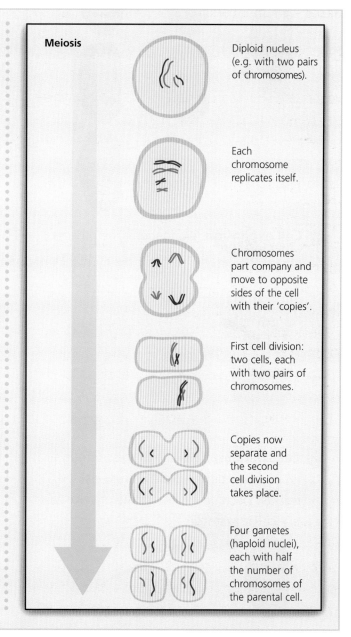

Meiosis

Diploid nucleus (e.g. with two pairs of chromosomes).

Each chromosome replicates itself.

Chromosomes part company and move to opposite sides of the cell with their 'copies'.

First cell division: two cells, each with two pairs of chromosomes.

Copies now separate and the second cell division takes place.

Four gametes (haploid nuclei), each with half the number of chromosomes of the parental cell.

Divide and Develop

Growth

Growth is a permanent increase in the size of an organism. There are three stages which contribute to the growth and development of organisms:

1. **Cell division**: the process in which two cells are formed from one (see mitosis p.11). For example...

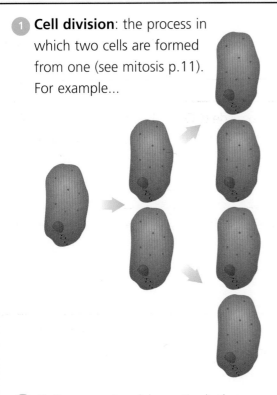

2. **Cell expansion** (elongation): the process in which cells, mainly in plants, elongate (stretch out). The actual cells get bigger, rather than reproduce. For example...

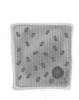  

3. **Cell specialisation**: the process through which an undifferentiated (unspecialised) cell can become a specific type of cell (see p.15). For example...

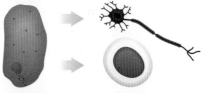

Measuring Growth

Although **length** (or height) is often used as a measure of growth (in plants and humans), it is not very accurate because it does not take into account growth in other directions, e.g. an increase in girth, width, or body mass. Growth is better measured by finding the **total mass** of an organism.

The best, and most accurate, way of doing this is to measure the **dry mass**. However, this can only be done when the organism is dead, because it involves heating the organism in an oven until all the water has evaporated out of it. As a result, **wet mass** is usually used as an alternative measure of growth. Measuring wet mass means measuring the total mass of a living organism.

Plants and animals grow in different ways:
- Plants continue to grow throughout their lives in height and width.
- Most animals grow quickly at first before slowing down. They eventually stop growing.

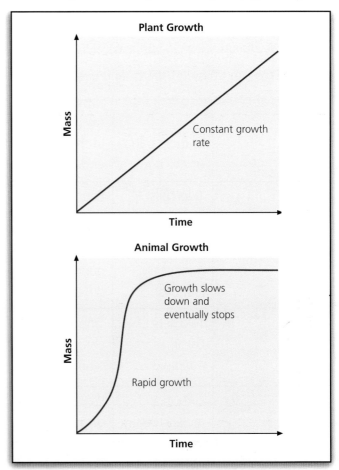

Divide and Develop

Nature and Nurture

'Nature versus nurture' describes the factors that can influence the growth of an organism.

Nature refers to the genes that are inherited from the parents. **Nurture** refers to environmental influences.

A good example is size. Size is a **continuous variable**, i.e. it can take any value within a range. For all species there is a limit to how large or small the organism can grow, but individuals will vary in size within that range.

In humans, height is a continuous variable. It is influenced by three factors:

1. **Genes** – if parents are tall then it is likely that their children will also be tall.
2. **Hormones** coordinate growth in the body, for example, they stimulate mitosis in bones, causing them to grow.
3. **Nutrition** – for example, a healthy, balanced diet will allow an individual to achieve their full potential size (determined by genes and hormones).

The graph below shows how height can vary within a group of people of the same age.

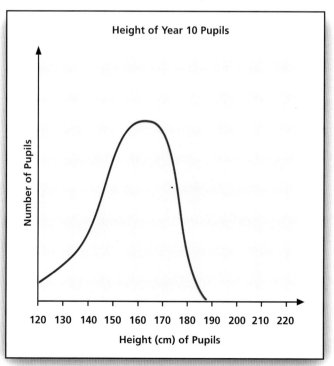

Height of Year 10 Pupils

Number of Pupils (vertical axis)

Height (cm) of Pupils: 120 130 140 150 160 170 180 190 200 210 220

Growth and Distribution of Plants

Genes influence the size of plants. In addition, plants need various resources to live and grow properly:

Resource	How do plants get it?
Light – for photosynthesis.	Absorb it through their leaves. Light
Carbon dioxide (CO_2) – for photosynthesis.	Absorb it from the air through their leaves. CO_2
Oxygen (O_2) – for respiration.	Absorb it from the air through their leaves. O_2
Nutrients (nitrates and phosphates) – for healthy growth and development.	Roots absorb these from the soil.
Temperature (warmth) – drives the plant's metabolism.	From the surrounding environment.

Plants will only grow in places where they are able to get the right environmental resources. For example, if a habitat is very shaded, very little light can get through, meaning plants will tend not to grow there. Plants that are able to survive in such places are specially adapted to cope with low light conditions.

Plants produce **hormones**, which make their roots grow down into the soil and their shoots grow up into the air. Gardeners and farmers sometimes use artificial hormones to try to make the plants grow better.

Divide and Develop

Artificial Plant Hormones

Auxins are naturally occurring plant hormones which control the **fruit initiation**, i.e. the development of fruit.

To ensure that fruit is available all year round, fruit growers spray unpollinated flowers with **synthetic auxin**. This will make the plants produce fruit without fertilisation occurring. As a result, the fruits do not contain seeds (pips).

Another plant hormone, called **ethene**, is used to make fruit ripen. For example, bananas are picked whilst they are still green and unripe. Ethene is used to ripen the bananas during transportation so that they are ready for sale in the shops.

Performance-enhancing Drugs

There are drugs that act on the body in a similar way to natural growth hormones. In the context of sport, these drugs are classed as **performance-enhancing drugs** because their effects can increase the body mass and strength of an athlete and, therefore, potentially improve their performance.

Professional sport is highly competitive and athletes face enormous pressure. Performance-enhancing drugs are banned in all sports, because their use does not represent the athlete's true ability, and therefore makes the competition unfair. However, athletes sometimes risk using them, for a number of reasons:

- to recover from an injury more quickly
- to mask pain so they can continue to perform
- to be the best and win at all costs
- to make the most of their short sports career
- to improve on their natural ability (which can help them to attract better sponsorship deals)
- to reap the financial rewards (professional athletes can earn huge salaries, and prizes often include large sums of money).

Anabolic steroids, for example, have a similar effect on the body as the male hormone testosterone; they stimulate the development of muscle tissue.

Some athletes claim that they help their performance by increasing their muscle strength, by allowing them to train harder and for longer, and by increasing their desire to win (psychological effect).

However, there are many health problems associated with the use of anabolic steroids, including liver disorders, heart disease, reduced sperm production in males (sometimes leading to sterility), and altered behaviour such as increased aggression and / or moodiness.

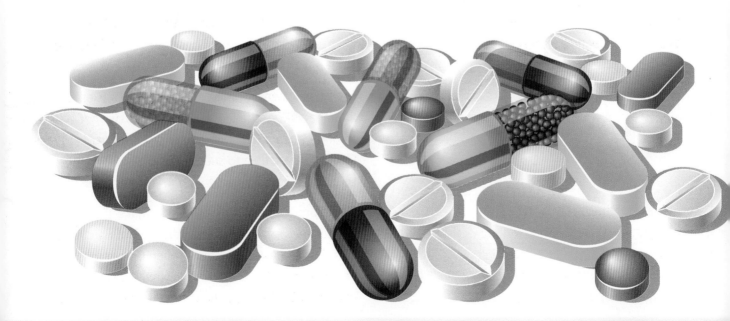

Regeneration in Animals

Plants have the ability to **regenerate** new leaves and branches (or side shoots) if old ones are lost.

In animals, however, the regeneration of body parts is rare: most animals cannot regenerate lost body parts. Animals that *can* replace body parts generally do so as part of a **defence mechanism**, i.e. they can sacrifice certain body parts to escape capture by a predator and then grow new ones. For example...

- **worms** – if an earthworm is cut in half, each half will regenerate the missing half. Flatworms (planarians) can be cut into several pieces and each section will regenerate into a complete flatworm
- **spiders** – immature spiders can re-grow legs when they shed their skin (exoskeleton). An adult spider is not able to re-grow any body parts
- **reptiles** – lizards can shed their tails and even legs, then re-grow them.

Studying regeneration in animals helps scientists to understand more about stems cells and how they might be used in medicine.

Stem Cells

Most cells are specialised to allow them to perform a particular job efficiently. The process by which they become specialised is called **differentiation**.

Plant cells can differentiate at any time, whereas animal cells only tend to differentiate soon after they are made. Animal stem cells can differentiate into all other types of cells. However, they lose the ability to differentiate as the animal matures.

Stem cells are undifferentiated (i.e. unspecialised). This means that they could, theoretically, differentiate into any type of cell. Research has been carried out which shows that stem cells could potentially be used to replace damaged cells and tissues to help in the treatment of diseases.

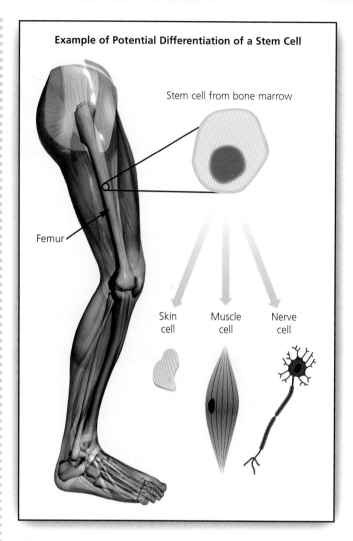

Example of Potential Differentiation of a Stem Cell

Stem cell from bone marrow

Femur

Skin cell

Muscle cell

Nerve cell

The Hayflick Limit

In 1965, Dr Leonard Hayflick discovered that there is a limit to how many times a differentiated cell can divide by mitosis. This is known as the **Hayflick limit**.

In human cells the Hayflick limit is about 52 divisions. As cells approach this limit they begin to show signs of old age.

Stem cells have not differentiated, which means that they have no Hayflick limit. So, they continue to divide throughout the whole of the organism's life. In terms of using stem cells to treat disease, this is a real benefit; doctors could generate lots of specialised cells from just a few stem cells.

Cancer cells also have no Hayflick limit. This means that doctors have to eliminate all the cancerous cells to successfully treat the patient, which is why it is important to diagnose the disease in the early stages.

Divide and Develop

Selective Breeding

For a farmer to make a profit, the animals and crop plants must be efficient at producing food. This means producing high-quality food, large quantities of food, or both, through **selective breeding (artificial selection)**. For example...

- **Increasing quality** – Jersey cows have been selectively bred over many generations to produce high-fat milk. Its rich creaminess means that it can be sold for a higher price than 'ordinary' milk.
- **Increasing quantity (numbers)** – sheep that produce twins are very desirable because the farmer gets twice as many animals. Some animals are more likely to produce twins than others because of their genes; it is an inherited trait. So, it is a characteristic that is selected by breeders.
- **Increasing yield** – dwarf wheat plants are sturdier than normal wheat plants, and put less energy into the growth of their stems (the bit that eventually becomes straw). Consequently, wheat can be bred to produce dwarf plants with high yielding seed-heads to maximise cost-effectiveness.

Cloning

It is possible to clone mammals (i.e. produce organisms with identical genetic information) by the process shown in the diagram opposite.

In 1996, at the Roslyn Institute, near Edinburgh, Dolly the sheep was cloned using this technique. Scientists believe that one possible danger of cloning in this way is premature ageing. Sheep normally live to 16 years of age. However, Dolly had to be put down when she was six because she was suffering from arthritis and lung disease – conditions normally associated with older sheep.

Because the egg cell receives genetic information from just one parent (rather than receiving copies of genes from two parents), defects in the DNA are more likely to affect the overall organisation of cells and tissues during the development of cloned embryos and, therefore, lead to abnormalities (e.g. in brain structure).

Scientific evidence suggests that there are risks associated with the later stages of embryonic development of clones. Many embryos do not even survive until birth. The Roslyn Institute scientists tried 276 times before they were successful with Dolly.

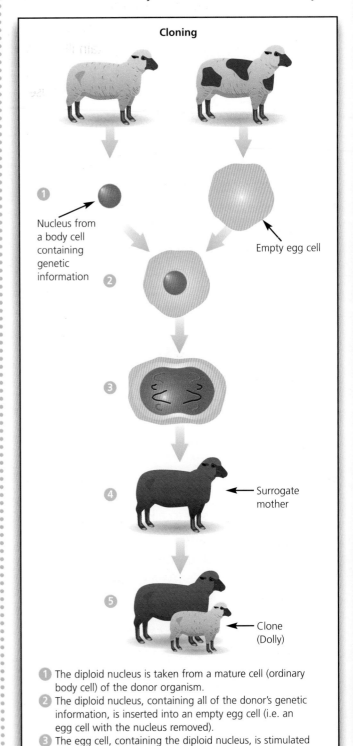

Cloning

Nucleus from a body cell containing genetic information

Empty egg cell

Surrogate mother

Clone (Dolly)

1. The diploid nucleus is taken from a mature cell (ordinary body cell) of the donor organism.
2. The diploid nucleus, containing all of the donor's genetic information, is inserted into an empty egg cell (i.e. an egg cell with the nucleus removed).
3. The egg cell, containing the diploid nucleus, is stimulated so that it begins to divide by mitosis.
4. The resulting embryo is placed in the uterus of a 'surrogate mother'.
5. The embryo develops into a foetus and is born as normal.

The Genetic Debate

In recent years, scientists have made great advances in understanding genes, chromosomes and inheritance:

- we know that genes control characteristics
- we know that genes are inherited
- we can determine if an individual's genes will make them more susceptible to certain illnesses, e.g. breast cancer
- we may soon be able to remove genes and use them to replace 'faulty' genes, which cause genetic disorders.

However, some people are very concerned about the **ethical issues** that this new-found understanding raises. Some concerns include…

- the possibility of 'designer babies', i.e. parents may be able to select the characteristics of their offspring (e.g. sex, eye colour)
- the possibility that insurance companies could use genetic screening to refuse to cover individuals with an increased risk of disease
- the possibility of increased abortion rates.

N.B. Ethical issues are concerned with what is morally right and wrong.

Gene Therapy

Gene therapy is the name given to an experimental technique that involves transplanting genes (DNA) into an individual's cells to help treat inherited diseases, such as cystic fibrosis.

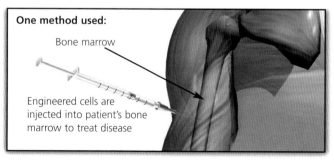

One method used:

Bone marrow

Engineered cells are injected into patient's bone marrow to treat disease

At the moment, gene therapy can only provide short-term relief from the symptoms of the disease. Because the new genes are only transferred into target body cells, not sex cells (sperm and ova), they cannot be passed on to offspring.

Missing or damaged genes can cause certain diseases, like cancer. It should, therefore, be possible to treat these diseases by inserting the missing gene or replacing the damaged one. At the moment, scientists are looking at how this can be achieved using **gene therapy**.

Researchers are also looking at alternative ways of using gene therapy to fight cancer…

- by introducing genes that will improve a patient's **immune response** to the disease
- by injecting cancer cells with genes that make them more sensitive to treatments
- by introducing genes that make healthy cells more resistant to the side effects of high doses of anti-cancer drugs
- by injecting cancer cells with 'suicide' genes that lead to the destruction of those cancer cells.

Legal Abortions

Most pregnant women in developed countries have an ultrasound scan. If a problem with the foetus is suspected, further tests are carried out. If a serious abnormality is detected, the woman is given the option of having an **abortion**. Abortion is the premature **termination** of a **pregnancy**. Some people believe abortion is wrong.

In humans, pregnancy lasts an average of 40 weeks. The legal time limit for an abortion is 24 weeks into the pregnancy. This limit is based on the survival chances of the foetus if it was born prematurely, i.e. if it was born 24 weeks into a pregnancy, a foetus would be very unlikely to be developed enough to survive.

However, some groups of people want the limit to be reduced to 18 weeks. They argue that a 24-week old foetus can experience pain and can respond to sound; its brain is growing quickly and most body systems are fully functional. Other 'pro-life' groups believe that abortion should be made illegal altogether.

Divide and Develop

Glossary

Cancer cell – a cell that divides uncontrollably to eventually form a tumour

Cell division – the process by which a cell splits to produce new cells

Chromosome – a long strand of genes made from DNA

Continuous variation – variation in a feature that can have an infinite number of values within a range, e.g. human height

Differentiation – the process by which a cell becomes specialised to perform a specific function

Diploid – a nucleus of a cell which contains two sets of chromosomes: normal body cells (not gametes)

Elongation – when a plant cell becomes longer during the process of differentiation

Embryo – a growing cluster of cells; the first stage in the development of an unborn baby

Foetus – the development from an embryo, usually about seven weeks after fertilisation. In humans, bone cells start to become visible

Gametes – sex cells; eggs / ova and sperms

Gene – a section of DNA which controls a particular feature

Genetic modification – altering the normal, or natural, genetic make-up of an organism

Growth – the permanent increase in the size of an organism

Haploid – a nucleus of a cell which contains one set of chromosomes, e.g. gametes (eggs and sperms)

Hormones – chemical messengers produced by the endocrine glands and transported by the blood to particular target cells or organs

Inheritance – the process by which characteristics are passed on from one generation to the next

Mitosis – a type of division in a cell's nucleus which produces new diploid cells for growth, or to replace damaged and worn out cells

Nucleus – the part of a cell which contains the chromosomes; it is surrounded by a membrane

Nutrient – a chemical compound needed by living things for the healthy production of new cells (e.g. vitamins, minerals, proteins).

Ovum (**Ova** – plural) – egg cell; female sex cell

Regeneration – the replacement of body parts by growing new ones

Selective breeding – the artificial selection of individual organisms for breeding based on their desirable characteristics

Species – a group of organisms that can breed amongst themselves and produce fertile offspring

Sperm – male sex cell

Stem cell – an undifferentiated cell which has the potential to develop into a specialised cell

Termination – bringing to an end, as in abortion (ending) of pregnancy

> (HT) **Meiosis** – a type of division in a cell's nucleus which produces sex cells (gametes)

Biospheres

The **biosphere** is the part of the Earth and its atmosphere where life exists.

Scientists can build an artificial biosphere (which would look something like one of the biomes (domes) at the Eden Project in Cornwall). An artificial biosphere is a structure designed to sustain life in a place which otherwise would not have life.

Some scientists believe that an artificial biosphere on another planet, such as Mars, would be a way to colonise the planet. For this to work, the biosphere would have to be self-contained and therefore sustainable. Amongst other things, the biosphere would have to have…

- enough photosynthesising plants to supply oxygen and food
- the ability to recycle all waste materials
- a method of keeping warm (the surface temperature on Mars is between -120°C and 25°C
- a method of melting Martian ice.

Comparing Plant and Animal Cells

All living organisms are made up of cells. The structures of different types of cells are related to their functions.

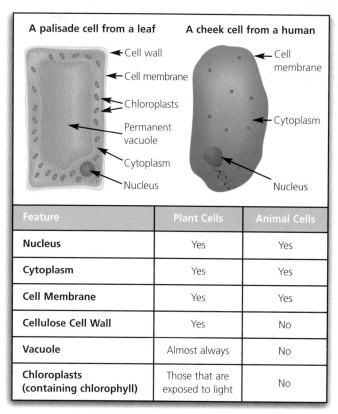

A palisade cell from a leaf — Cell wall, Cell membrane, Chloroplasts, Permanent vacuole, Cytoplasm, Nucleus

A cheek cell from a human — Cell membrane, Cytoplasm, Nucleus

Feature	Plant Cells	Animal Cells
Nucleus	Yes	Yes
Cytoplasm	Yes	Yes
Cell Membrane	Yes	Yes
Cellulose Cell Wall	Yes	No
Vacuole	Almost always	No
Chloroplasts (containing chlorophyll)	Those that are exposed to light	No

How Green Plants Make Food

Plants make their own food by the process of **photosynthesis**. Photosynthesis means 'making through light'. It occurs in the **chloroplasts** of the many cells of green plants that are exposed to light (mainly in the leaves).

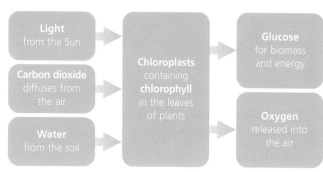

Light from the Sun → Chloroplasts containing chlorophyll in the leaves of plants → Glucose for biomass and energy

Carbon dioxide diffuses from the air →

Water from the soil → → Oxygen released into the air

Reactants	⟶	Products

$$\text{Carbon dioxide} + \text{Water} \xrightarrow[\text{Chlorophyll}]{\text{Light}} \text{Glucose} + \text{Oxygen}$$

$$6CO_2 + 6H_2O \xrightarrow[\text{Chlorophyll}]{\text{Light}} C_6H_{12}O_6 + 6O_2$$

Energy Flow

Factors Affecting Photosynthesis

Temperature, carbon dioxide concentration and **light intensity** interact to affect the rate of photosynthesis. Any one of them, at a particular time, may be the **limiting factor**.

Effect of Temperature

1. As the temperature rises so does the rate of photosynthesis. This means temperature is limiting the rate of photosynthesis.
2. As the temperature exceeds 37°C, the enzymes controlling photosynthesis start to be destroyed and the rate of photosynthesis drops to zero.

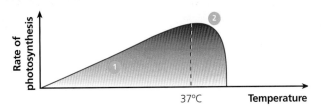

Effect of Carbon Dioxide Concentration

1. As the carbon dioxide concentration rises so does the rate of photosynthesis. So carbon dioxide is limiting the rate of photosynthesis.
2. The rise in carbon dioxide levels now has no effect. Carbon dioxide is no longer the limiting factor. Light or temperature must now be the limiting factor.

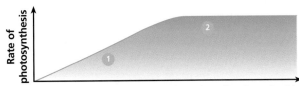

Effect of Light Intensity

1. As the light intensity increases so does the rate of photosynthesis. This means light intensity is limiting the rate of photosynthesis.
2. The rise in light intensity now has no effect. Light is no longer the limiting factor. Carbon dioxide or temperature must now be the limiting factor.

Absorbing Mineral Salts

Plants absorb mineral salts (including nitrates and phosphates) from the soil, through their root hairs. Mineral salts are sometimes called ions, mineral ions, salts or minerals.

Because plants absorb mineral salts against a concentration gradient (i.e. from the low concentration of minerals in the soil to the high concentration of minerals inside the root hair) they do this by **active transport**. This means that the plant must use energy from respiration to absorb the minerals. Plants need minerals for healthy growth.

Root Hair Cell

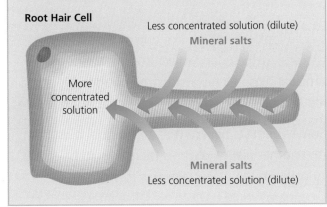

Uses For Plants

We use plants for all sorts of things:

Part of Plant	Uses
Flowers	• Food, e.g. broccoli. • Decorations, e.g. bunches of flowers.
Stem	• Food, e.g. celery. • Building materials, e.g. wood, bamboo.
Leaves	• Food, e.g. lettuce, cabbage. • Building materials (e.g. for roofs of huts in developing countries).
Roots	• Food, e.g. carrots, parsnips, beetroot.

The Carbon Cycle

Carbon is an element that forms the basis of all living things. On Earth, the processes by which materials are removed by living things should, ideally, be balanced by processes which return them, so these materials can be recycled. The constant recycling of carbon is called the **carbon cycle**.

Plants and animals respire all the time. However, during daylight hours, plants also photosynthesise.

The amount of oxygen that plants use for respiration is only a tiny fraction of the amount they produce during photosynthesis. This means that the oxygen consumed by animals is more than adequately replaced by photosynthesis in normal circumstances. However, the levels of oxygen and carbon dioxide in the atmosphere depend upon the fine balance between respiration and photosynthesis being maintained.

Human activity, such as the burning of fossil fuels and deforestation is starting to upset this balance.

The four main processes in the carbon cycle are as follows (see diagram below):

1. **Photosynthesis** – carbon dioxide is **removed** from the atmosphere by green plants to produce glucose. Some is returned to the air by the plants during respiration.

2. **Respiration** – plants and animals respire, **releasing** carbon dioxide into the atmosphere.

3. **Decay** – when plants and animals die, other animals and microorganisms feed on their bodies, causing them to break down, **releasing** carbon dioxide into the air. As the animals and microorganisms eat the dead plants and animals they respire, releasing carbon dioxide into the air.

4. **Combustion** – fossil fuels that are burned in power stations **release** carbon dioxide into the atmosphere.

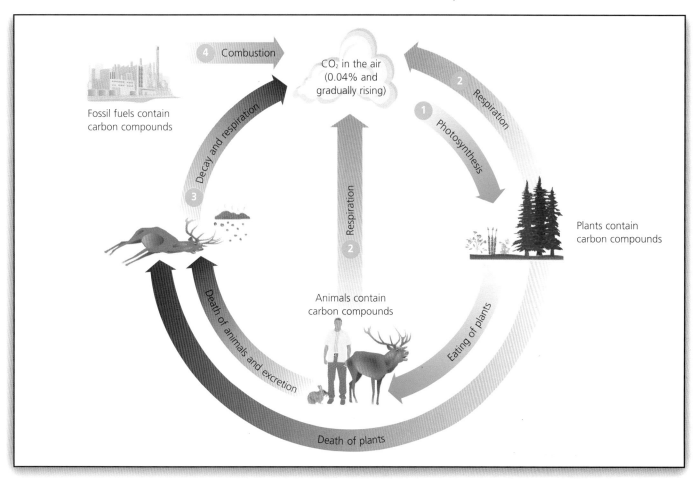

Energy Flow

The Nitrogen Cycle

The **nitrogen cycle** shows how nitrogen and its compounds are recycled in nature. It is a vital element of all living things and is used to make proteins. Proteins are used in plant and animal growth. All enzymes are proteins. Bacteria play an important role in the nitrogen cycle. The main processes in the nitrogen cycle are as follows:

1. **Nitrogen-fixing bacteria** convert atmospheric nitrogen into nitrates in soil. Some of these bacteria live in the soil, whilst others are found in the roots of leguminous plants (e.g. pea plants).

2. When plants are eaten the nitrogen becomes animal protein.

3. Dead organisms and waste contain ammonium compounds.

4. **Decomposers** convert urea, faeces and protein from dead organisms into ammonium compounds.

5. **Nitrifying bacteria** convert ammonium compounds into nitrates in the soil.

6. **Denitrifying bacteria** convert nitrates into atmospheric nitrogen and ammonium compounds.

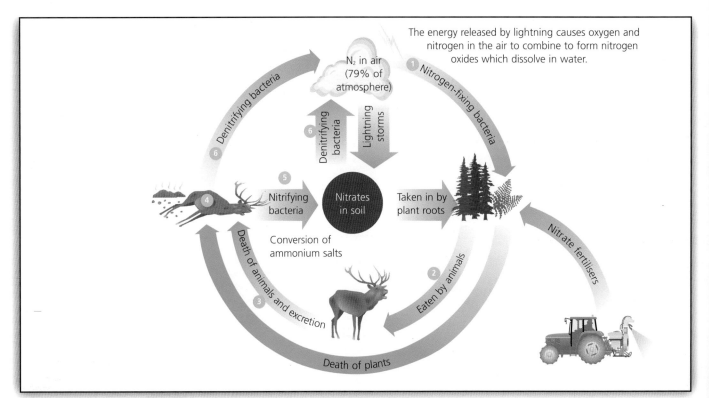

Nitrogenous Fertilisers

Plants need nitrogen for healthy growth, but they cannot use the nitrogen from the air because it is **inert** (unreactive). Farmers use fertilisers to replace the nitrogen in the soil which has been used up by crops. This means that crop yields can be increased. But **indiscriminate** (careless) use of fertilisers can lead to environmental damage and **eutrophication**, illustrated below.

Nitrates cause excessive algal growth which blocks off sunlight to other plants

The other plants cannot photosynthesise so they die and start to rot

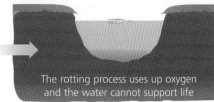

The rotting process uses up oxygen and the water cannot support life

The Greenhouse Effect and Global Warming

Heat energy from the Sun reaches the Earth. Without this heat energy, the Earth would be far too cold for life to exist. **Carbon dioxide** and **methane** in the atmosphere act as an **insulating layer** around the Earth, which means that a lot of this heat is kept in. This is called the **Greenhouse Effect**. Carbon dioxide and methane are therefore known as **greenhouse gases**.

However, the levels of these insulating gases are increasing, which is resulting in more heat energy being kept inside the Earth's atmosphere. This is leading to **global warming**.

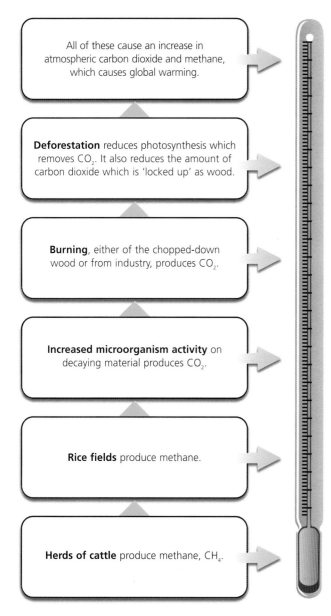

All of these cause an increase in atmospheric carbon dioxide and methane, which causes global warming.

Deforestation reduces photosynthesis which removes CO_2. It also reduces the amount of carbon dioxide which is 'locked up' as wood.

Burning, either of the chopped-down wood or from industry, produces CO_2.

Increased microorganism activity on decaying material produces CO_2.

Rice fields produce methane.

Herds of cattle produce methane, CH_4.

The amounts of greenhouse gases in the atmosphere are increasing as a result of an increase in the human population. Humans have been using the Earth's resources **unsustainably**, i.e. with no consideration for future generations, and this is leading to massive environmental change. For example, **deforestation** (the large-scale cutting down of trees for timber, and to provide land for agriculture) has led to…

- an increase in the amount of carbon dioxide released into the atmosphere due to wood burning and wood decay by microorganisms
- a reduction in the rate at which carbon dioxide is removed from the atmosphere by photosynthesis.

Global Warming

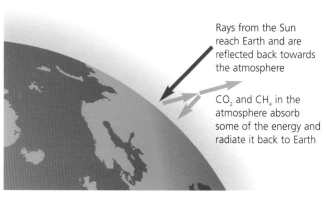

Rays from the Sun reach Earth and are reflected back towards the atmosphere

CO_2 and CH_4 in the atmosphere absorb some of the energy and radiate it back to Earth

If the average temperature of the Earth increases by just a few degrees, millions of people around the world will be affected because there will be…
- substantial climate changes
- a rise in sea levels.

Energy Flow

Food Production and Distribution

In the past, food production was a local issue. People produced the food they needed for themselves. Today, however, it is quite different.

Some countries (**developed countries**) produce lots of food and their inhabitants are well fed. There is a constant, plentiful supply of food, lots of choice and competitive prices at which to buy the food. However, this can also be a problem; for example, in many developed countries, people eat too much food which has a high fat and / or salt content. This can lead to **obesity** and a range of associated health problems including **heart disease**, **diabetes** (high blood sugar) and **arthritis** (worn joints).

On the other hand, in many parts of the world (**developing countries**), there is not enough food. In these countries, the conditions for growing food are not good (e.g. hot and dry with little rainfall) and they cannot afford to buy food from other countries. People suffer from **malnutrition** and other problems such as reduced resistance to infection. Hundreds of thousands of people die from **starvation** each year.

Some solutions to the problem of unequal food distribution include...

- sending food from richer countries to poorer countries. However, the food would take a long time to get there, and it would be a very expensive process (transport costs etc.)
- teaching people how to produce their own food. However, conditions in these countries are often poor meaning many crops fail.

Maximising Food Production

Energy transfer can be maximised in food production. Professionals who are responsible for food production are able to maximise how much food is produced by using designated food production plants such as **fish farms** and **large greenhouses**. The produce is encouraged to grow in a **controlled environment** providing the optimum temperature, correct nutrients, plentiful supply of water etc.

Fish Farms

In Britain, most of the salmon and trout that we eat comes from fish farms. Fish farms consist of large cages suspended in lakes / lochs. The fish are encouraged to grow by...

- keeping eggs and very young fish in tanks until they can fend for themselves
- giving them a high-protein diet
- keeping predators away
- using chemicals to combat pests (parasites) and disease.

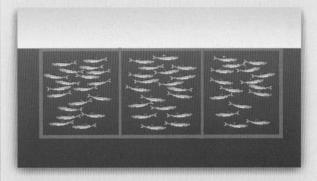

Greenhouses

The conditions in greenhouses can be controlled (often using computerised systems) to provide optimum growing conditions for the crop plants being cultivated. These conditions would include...

- optimum conditions for photosynthesis (optimum light, CO_2 and temperature)
- plenty of water
- appropriate use of pesticides and herbicides
- use of fertilisers
- growing plants that naturally produce large crops.

Glossary

Animal cell – the basic structural and functional unit of animals; typically consists of a nucleus surrounded by cytoplasm containing mitochondria and surrounded by a cell membrane

Biosphere – the part of the Earth which can support life

Carbon cycle – the process by which carbon is recycled between living organisms and the environment; it also includes the carbon that is produced as the result of combustion

Cellulose (cell wall) – cellulose is a carbohydrate which forms walls in plant cells. It provides the cells with structural support

Chlorophyll – green photosynthetic chemical found in chloroplasts, which absorbs light for photosynthesis

Chloroplast – an organelle found in the green parts of plants; contains the green photosynthetic chemical chlorophyll

Combustion – process by which fuel is burned to release heat energy; produces carbon dioxide

Cytoplasm – everything inside a cell that is not the nucleus or other organelles

Denitrifying bacteria – bacteria which release nitrogen from nitrogen-containing compounds

Decomposer – organisms (typically bacteria and fungi) that break down dead animals and plants

Deforestation – the cutting down of very large areas of forests (typically rainforests)

Disease – an illness caused by a microorganism, environmental change, or 'faulty' genes

Fertilisers – chemicals that typically contain nitrates, phosphates and potassium. They are added to the soil to replace the chemicals that are used by plants

Food production – the process by which food is cultivated or grown

Global warming – the increase in the average temperature on Earth, due to a rise in levels of greenhouse gases in the atmosphere

Glucose – a carbohydrate, sometimes referred to as a simple sugar; product of photosynthesis

Membrane – surrounds cells and controls the movement of chemicals and particles into and out of the cell

Microorganism – (same as microbe) an organism that can only be seen with a microscope, e.g. bacteria

Mineral salt – chemicals needed by living organisms to live and stay healthy; also known as ions, mineral ions, salts and minerals

Nitrifying bacteria – bacteria that convert ammonium compounds into nitrates; an important part of the nitrogen cycle

Nitrogen cycle – the process by which nitrogen is recycled between living organisms and the environment

Nitrogen-fixing bacteria – bacteria that make nitrates from atmospheric nitrogen; an important part of the nitrogen cycle

Nucleus – the part of a cell which is surrounded by a membrane and contains the chromosomes. It controls the activities of the cell

Photosynthesis – the process by which green plants use light energy to make glucose

Plant cell – the basic structural and functional unit of plants; typically consists of a nucleus surrounded by cytoplasm containing mitochondria and chloroplasts, a cell membrane and a cellulose cell wall

Predator – an animal that hunts, kills and eats what it kills (prey)

Respiration – a series of chemical reactions by which living organisms obtain energy from food

Root – part of a plant that (usually) grows into the soil. Roots absorb water and minerals as well as anchoring the plant

Vacuole – a large space in the centre of a plant cell which is full of cell sap

HT **Active transport** – requires energy to move molecules, against a concentration gradient, from an area of low concentration to an area of high concentration

Interdependence

Interdependence

Interdependence refers to a **relationship** between living organisms where organisms **depend** on each other for some resource or for survival. What happens to one organism will affect what happens to other organisms: everything is dependent on everything else.

Competition

There is **competition** between members of the same species, or members of different species, when they both need the same resource to survive.

Plants' Needs

- Leaves need space to absorb sunlight to photosynthesise.
- Roots need soil space to absorb minerals and water.

Animals' Needs

- Animals need space to breed and build a home (nest), and territory for hunting.
- Herbivores need plants to eat.
- Carnivores need animals to eat.

More successful plants and animals tend to produce more offspring (seeds or babies).

Predation

Predators are animals that **kill** and **eat** other animals, called **prey**. There is a cycle between the numbers of predators and the numbers of prey:

1. When the **prey population** is large, the **predator population** will **increase** in number.
2. When the **predator population** is large, lots of prey will be eaten and the **prey numbers** will **fall**.
3. When the **prey population** is small, the **predator population** will fall.

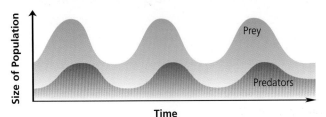

Adaptation

Adaptations are special **features** or types of **behaviour** which make a living organism well-suited to its environment.

Adaptations **develop** as the result of **evolution**. They increase an organism's chance of staying alive.

Adaptations are **biological solutions** to the challenge of **survival**.

Examples of Adaptations

A Cold Terrestrial Climate – Polar Bear

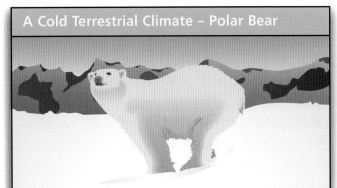

- Small surface area to volume ratio to reduce heat loss.
- Large amount of insulating fat beneath skin.
- Large feet to spread its weight on the ice.
- Powerful legs so it can swim to catch food.
- White coat so it is camouflaged.

A Hot Terrestrial Climate – Camel

- Large surface area to volume ratio to increase heat loss.
- Body fat stored in hump (almost no fat beneath skin).
- Sandy coat so it is camouflaged.
- Loses very little water through urine and sweating.
- Can drink up to 20 gallons of water at once.

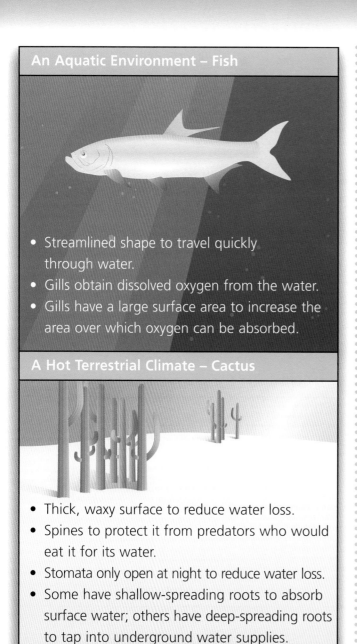

An Aquatic Environment – Fish

- Streamlined shape to travel quickly through water.
- Gills obtain dissolved oxygen from the water.
- Gills have a large surface area to increase the area over which oxygen can be absorbed.

A Hot Terrestrial Climate – Cactus

- Thick, waxy surface to reduce water loss.
- Spines to protect it from predators who would eat it for its water.
- Stomata only open at night to reduce water loss.
- Some have shallow-spreading roots to absorb surface water; others have deep-spreading roots to tap into underground water supplies.

An Aquatic Environment – Water Lily

- Flexible stem so that it can bend in the water's current.
- Underwater leaves are streamlined.
- Leaves often grow on the surface of the water so that they can photosynthesise.

Extreme Habitats

Different living things are adapted to live in all parts of the world. Some habitats on Earth are described as **extreme**. Organisms living in extreme habitats need to have very special adaptations to be able to survive. Some examples are given below:

Deep Sea Volcanic Vents

Often found under the oceans, they discharge very hot water (400°C and above). As it is completely dark, there are no photosynthesising plants. However, there are many different types of organisms that are adapted to survive here by...

- being able to cope with the high pressure and temperature
- having very highly developed senses other than sight.

The Antarctic

The temperatures are very low: they can fall to below -50°C. Not many animals can survive in such difficult conditions. However, penguins are adapted to survive because they...

- have a compact shape, meaning that relatively little heat is lost through the surface
- have a thick layer of insulating fat under the skin
- have very tightly packed, waterproof feathers for insulation
- often huddle in large, tightly packed groups (rookeries): they constantly move into the centre so that the ones on the outside are not there for long and, therefore, never get too cold.

High Altitudes (Mountain Tops)

Being at, or living at, high altitudes means conditions are very cold and windy, and there is little or no food. There is also a shortage of oxygen.

The density of air (and hence oxygen) decreases the higher you go. So, people have to 'acclimatise' by spending time at progressively higher altitudes. This allows the body to produce extra red blood cells to capture as much oxygen as possible to transport around the body, allowing people to live in high altitude habitats.

Interdependence

Pollution

Pollution is the contamination of the environment by **waste substances**, produced as the result of **human activity**.

Many waste substances are formed from the burning of fossil fuels to produce energy.

Air pollution may consist of...

Hydrocarbons

- Released from combustion of fossil fuels (vehicles and factories).

Carbon Dioxide

- Released from combustion of fossil fuels (vehicles and factories).
- An important 'greenhouse gas'.

Sulphur Dioxide

- Released from combustion of fossil fuels (vehicles and factories).
- Contributes to acid rain.

Carbon Monoxide

- Released from vehicle exhausts and from many heavy industries.

Water pollution may consist of...

Sewage (Human Waste)

- Bacteria feed on it and use up all the oxygen in the water. This causes other living things (e.g. water plants and fish) to die of asphyxiation (lack of oxygen).
- Contributes to eutrophication.

Nitrates (Found in Fertilisers)

- Can be washed out of the soil into streams, rivers, ponds and lakes.
- Cause water plants to grow excessively. When the plants die they are fed on by bacteria, which use up all the oxygen in the water. This causes other living things (e.g. water plants and fish) to die of asphyxiation (lack of oxygen.) (This is eutrophication.)

Phosphates (Found in Waste Water from Laundries and run-off from Fields)

- Constituent of fertiliser (as in KPN fertilisers – the P stands for phosphates).
- Contributes to eutrophication.

Effects of Human Activity

Economic and industrial conditions influence and direct how human activity affects natural populations and the environment in different parts of the world:

1. **Land use:**
   - for building houses, roads, factories, schools etc.
   - farm land and the use of chemical fertilisers and pesticides
   - quarrying for rock.
2. **Use of raw materials:**
   - natural gas
   - crude oil
   - coal
   - metal ores.
3. **Waste:**
   - landfill sites
   - pollution (in the air, on land and in water).

All these activities have the effect of changing natural habitats and reducing the numbers of naturally occurring populations.

Some nations have more impact than others; developed, highly industrialised countries actually produce less air pollution overall than industrially developing countries. This is because developed countries have enforced guidelines and regulations for harmful emissions over the last few decades. However, in developing countries, the increase in levels of air pollution is a result of recent industrial development and economic growth.

Environmental Changes

It is important to protect natural **habitats** in order to protect the populations that live there. However, pollution changes habitats, so the naturally occurring populations of organisms either move away from the polluted habitat, or stay there and die. They could evolve (adapt) to cope with the changes but, in a short timescale, this is not possible. Therefore, to prevent a species becoming endangered, or even extinct, it is vital to protect its environment.

Sometimes, new populations move into a polluted area. These new populations are able to do this because they can cope with the pollution: they are already adapted.

Air Pollution Indicators

Lichen populations are very sensitive to sulphur dioxide air pollution and even quite low levels can kill them. This table displays some data collected from a polluted city. It shows the effect of an environmental change on the lichen population.

Distance from City Centre (km)	Number of Different Lichen Species	Sulphur Dioxide Levels (Arbitrary Units)
0	0	210
2	1	144
4	4	91
6	8	47
8	12	10
10	46	0

Few lichens indicate high concentration of sulphur dioxide in the air

Many lichens indicate low concentration of sulphur dioxide in the air

Interdependence

Conservation

Conservation keeps **ecosystems** stable as environmental conditions change. These conditions include both **biotic factors** (living things), and **abiotic factors** (temperature, humidity etc.).

Conservation can lead to greater **biodiversity** by...
- preventing species from becoming extinct
- maintaining variation within species
- preserving habitats.

Conservation management techniques include...
- **Reforestation** – the planting of forests on areas of land which are not currently forests. This provides new habitats.
- **Coppicing** – cutting young trees down at just above ground level to encourage the growth of side shoots; the process is repeated every few years. Trees with multiple trunks are produced.
- **Replacement planting** – planting trees to replace those that have been cut down. This maintains habitats.

Recycling

Recycling materials is now seen as a very important part of **sustainable development**, i.e. development that meets the needs of current generations without compromising the ability of future generations to meet their needs.

Local councils encourage us to recycle a range of materials including paper, plastic, metals and glass. Recycling reduces demand for raw materials and reduces the problems of waste disposal.

Global Temperature

The Earth's mean (average) temperature has been gradually increasing over the last two centuries, due to the Greenhouse Effect, caused by the increase in greenhouse gases. This increase is known as **global warming**.

HT Though the temperature rise is small, the effects of global warming could be devastating. This graph shows the rise in mean global temperature since 1880.

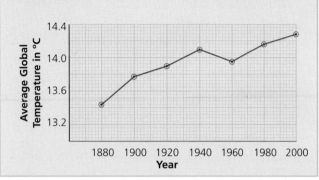

Global warming will cause flooding, changes in weather patterns, and droughts.

The Ozone Layer and Skin Cancer

Ozone is found in a thin layer above the Earth's atmosphere. It filters out some harmful ultraviolet (UV) radiation which can cause skin cancer.

Unfortunately, some of the ozone layer has been destroyed by chlorofluorocarbons (CFCs) and this has resulted in an increase in the amount of UV light reaching the Earth and, therefore, an increase in the number of cases of skin cancer.

The graphs below show that as the ozone layer has become thinner, cases of skin cancer have risen.

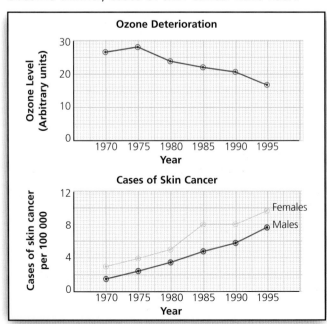

Interdependence

Glossary

Adaptation – a feature or a type of behaviour which makes an organism better suited to survive in its habitat

Aquatic – in water; i.e. a river, stream, pond or lake habitat

Biodiversity – the variety of different types of organisms in a habitat or ecosystem

Competition – the rivalry between members of the same species, or members of different species, for a resource that they both need

Conservation – the process by which ecosystems are kept stable as environmental conditions change; these conditions include both biotic (living things) and abiotic (temperature, light etc.) factors

Coppicing – cutting young trees down at just above ground level to encourage the growth of side shoots; the process is repeated every few years

Environment – the surroundings in which an organism lives

Extreme environment – a place where the living conditions for organisms are particularly harsh, e.g. the Antarctic (extreme cold)

Global temperature – the mean temperature of the Earth (taking into account the high temperatures in the tropics and the extremely low temperatures of the Polar regions)

Interdependence – the relationship between organisms where one organism depends on another for a resource

Nitrates – an important source of nitrogen for plants; nitrates are absorbed from the soil by the roots; constituent of many fertilisers, needed for healthy growth

Organism – a living thing

Ozone – O_3; found as a layer of gas in the upper atmosphere, ozone protects us from harmful UV rays by absorbing them

Phosphates – an important source of phosphorus for plants; phosphates are absorbed from the soil by the roots; constituent of many fertilisers, needed for healthy growth

Pollution – the contamination of an environment by chemicals, waste or heat that threatens existing habitats and / or endangers organisms

Population – a group of organisms of the same species living in a defined area

Predation – the process of predators hunting for prey

Recycling – the process by which resources are used again

Reforestation – the planting of forests on land which is not currently forest

Replacement planting – the planting of trees to replace those cut down

Resource – a raw material that is used by an organism

Sewage – human waste consisting of faeces and urine together with toilet paper and sanitary products which are flushed down toilets

Skin cancer – a disease which causes cells in the skin to divide uncontrollably to form tumours. Often caused by prolonged exposure to UV light

Terrestrial – on (dry) land, i.e. a land habitat

Waste disposal – the removal of rubbish

Synthesis

Balancing Equations

All chemical reactions follow the same simple rule: the mass of the reactants is equal to the mass of the products.

This means there must be the same number of atoms on both sides of the equation.

Number of atoms in reactants	=	Number of atoms in products

Writing Balanced Equations

If you are asked to write a balanced equation, follow these stages:

1. Write down the word equation for the reaction.
2. Write down the correct formula for each of the reactants and the products.
3. Check that there is the same number of each atom on both sides of the equation.
4. If the equation is already balanced, leave it. If the equation needs balancing write a number in front of one or more of the formulae. This increases the number of all of the atoms in that element or compound.
5. Make sure you include the state symbols:
   - (s) = solid
   - (l) = liquid
   - (g) = gas
   - (aq) = dissolved in water (aqueous solution).

Example

Balance the reaction between calcium carbonate and hydrochloric acid.

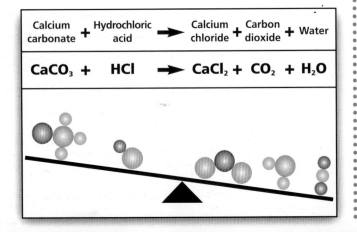

Calcium carbonate $+$ Hydrochloric acid $\rightarrow$ Calcium chloride $+$ Carbon dioxide $+$ Water

$CaCO_3 + HCl \rightarrow CaCl_2 + CO_2 + H_2O$

There are more chlorine atoms and hydrogen atoms on the products side than on the reactants side so, balance chlorine by doubling the amount of hydrochloric acid.

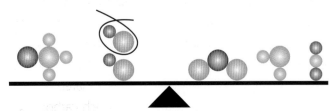

The amount of chlorine and hydrogen on both sides is now equal. This should now give you a balanced equation.

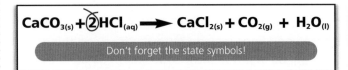

$$CaCO_{3(s)} + 2HCl_{(aq)} \rightarrow CaCl_{2(s)} + CO_{2(g)} + H_2O_{(l)}$$

Don't forget the state symbols!

Carbon Compounds

Carbon is an element found in Group 4 of the periodic table. This means that it has four electrons in its outer shell and therefore, it needs four more to complete its outer shell (see p.43). Therefore, carbon has the ability to form four bonds with other atoms.

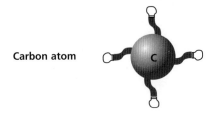

Carbon atom

This means that carbon atoms can bond together to make chains of (almost) unlimited size and complexity. Some bonds on the carbon atoms remain free to join with other atoms to form **carbon compounds**.

Carbon compounds are organic compounds that are the basis of life. They are found in all living things or are derived from living things. Examples include proteins, amino acids, carbohydrates and fats; compounds in fossil fuels; plastics; and pharmaceuticals made from fossil fuel compounds. The study of these carbon compounds is called **organic chemistry**.

Alkanes (Saturated Hydrocarbons)

A **hydrocarbon** is a compound containing hydrogen and carbon. The 'spine' of a hydrocarbon is made up of a chain of carbon atoms. When more than one carbon atom is present, they are joined by **single covalent carbon-carbon bonds**. A covalent bond is a very strong bond formed when electrons are shared between non-metal atoms (see p.49). Because each carbon atom is bonded to the maximum number of atoms, we say the hydrocarbon is **saturated**. It is known as an **alkane**.

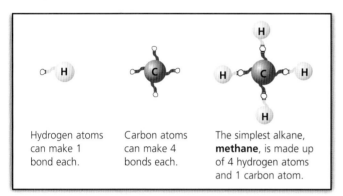

Hydrogen atoms can make 1 bond each.

Carbon atoms can make 4 bonds each.

The simplest alkane, **methane**, is made up of 4 hydrogen atoms and 1 carbon atom.

The next three simplest alkanes are **ethane, propane** and **butane**. Because they are saturated (i.e. the carbon atoms are all bonded to 4 other atoms), they are fairly unreactive although they do burn well.

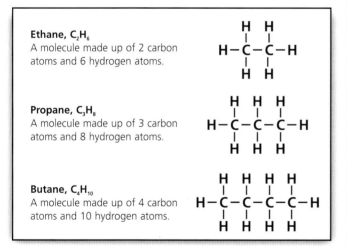

Ethane, C_2H_6
A molecule made up of 2 carbon atoms and 6 hydrogen atoms.

Propane, C_3H_8
A molecule made up of 3 carbon atoms and 8 hydrogen atoms.

Butane, C_4H_{10}
A molecule made up of 4 carbon atoms and 10 hydrogen atoms.

Alkenes (Unsaturated Hydrocarbons)

The **alkenes** are another kind of hydrocarbon. They are very similar to the alkanes, except that two of the carbon atoms are joined by a **double covalent carbon-carbon bond**. Because the carbon atoms are not bonded to the maximum number of atoms, we call them **unsaturated hydrocarbons**.

The simplest alkene is **ethene**, C_2H_4, which is made of 4 hydrogen atoms and 2 carbon atoms. Ethene contains 1 double carbon-carbon bond.

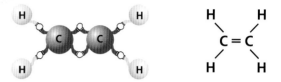

The next simplest alkene is **propene**, C_3H_6, which is made of 6 hydrogen atoms and 3 carbon atoms. Propene contains 1 double carbon-carbon bond and 1 single carbon-carbon bond.

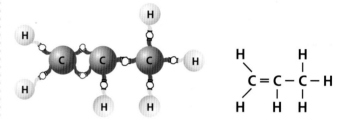

Testing for Alkanes and Alkenes

A simple test to distinguish between alkanes and alkenes is to add bromine water. Alkenes will **decolourise** bromine water as the alkene reacts with it. Alkanes have no effect on bromine water.

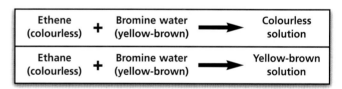

Ethene (colourless) +	Bromine water (yellow-brown) ⟶	Colourless solution
Ethane (colourless) +	Bromine water (yellow-brown) ⟶	Yellow-brown solution

HT Making Ethanol from Ethene

Ethene can be reacted with water in the presence of a catalyst (phosphoric acid) to produce **ethanol**.

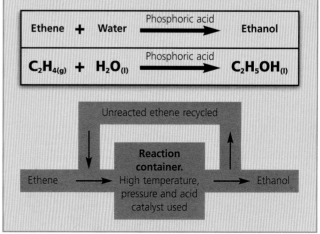

Ethene + Water	Phosphoric acid ⟶	Ethanol
$C_2H_{4(g)}$ + $H_2O_{(l)}$	Phosphoric acid ⟶	$C_2H_5OH_{(l)}$

Unreacted ethene recycled

Reaction container.
High temperature, pressure and acid catalyst used

Ethene

Ethanol

Synthesis

Cracking

Cracking involves the breaking down of long-chain hydrocarbons into more useful short-chain hydrocarbons, which release energy more quickly when burned.

Long-chain hydrocarbon

Short-chain hydrocarbons

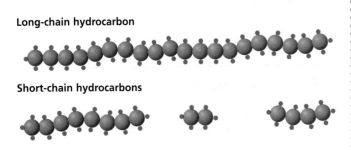

The long-chain hydrocarbon is heated until it vaporises. The vapour is then passed over a heated catalyst where a **thermal decomposition** reaction takes place.

In the laboratory, cracking can be carried out using the following apparatus:

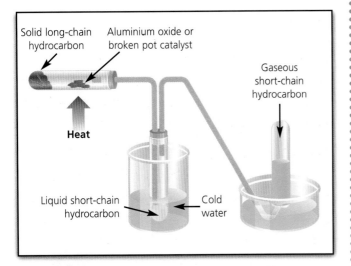

When alkanes are cracked, alkanes and alkenes are formed, for example…

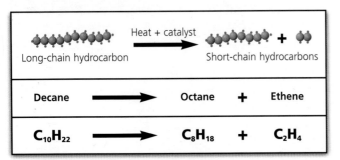

Monomers to Polymers

Polymers are long-chain molecules, formed from unsaturated **monomers**. A monomer is a short-chain hydrocarbon molecule. Monomers join together to form long-chain hydrocarbon molecules (polymers).

Monomers joining together to make polymers often do so through a condensation reaction. Some of the resulting polymers are used to make plastics.

Because alkenes are unsaturated, they are very good at joining together. When they join together without producing another substance, we call this **addition polymerisation**. For example, the formation of **poly(ethene)** from ethene:

Ethene monomers (unsaturated)	Poly(ethene) polymers (saturated)
$H\ \ \ H\ \ \ \ \ \ H\ \ \ H$	$H\ \ \ H\ \ \ H\ \ \ H$
$\ \|\ \ \ \|\ \ \ \ \ \ \ \|\ \ \ \|$	$\ \|\ \ \ \|\ \ \ \|\ \ \ \|$
$C=C\ \ +\ \ C=C\ \ +\ \ \longrightarrow$	$H-C-C-C-C-$
$\ \|\ \ \ \|\ \ \ \ \ \ \ \|\ \ \ \|$	$\ \|\ \ \ \|\ \ \ \|\ \ \ \|$
$H\ \ \ H\ \ \ \ \ \ H\ \ \ H$	$H\ \ \ H\ \ \ H\ \ \ H$
…and thousands more…	…and on and on…

Here is the general formula for addition polymerisation which can be used to represent the formation of a simple addition polymer:

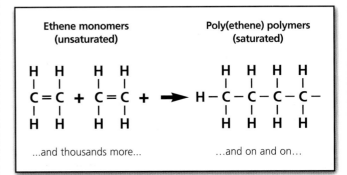

where n is a very large number

For example, if we take 'n' molecules of propene we can produce **poly(propene)**:

$$n\left(\begin{matrix}H & CH_3\\ | & |\\ C=C\\ | & |\\ H & H\end{matrix}\right)\xrightarrow[\text{Catalyst}]{\text{Pressure}}\left(\begin{matrix}H & CH_3\\ | & |\\ C-C\\ | & |\\ H & H\end{matrix}\right)_n$$

Properties of Polymers

Polymers have properties that make them very useful:
- they have good strength and elasticity
- they do not corrode
- they are good electrical and thermal insulators
- they have low densities
- they are colourful
- they can be easily moulded into shape.

Polymers can be divided into two groups: thermoplastics and thermosets (thermosetting plastics).

Thermoplastics can be easily softened and remoulded into new shapes.

Their polymer chains are held together in their structure by weak intermolecular forces which also give the material some rigidity and strength. However, these forces can be easily overcome by applying heat, which softens the polymer and enables it to be reformed as the chains slip easily over each other. It is not very rigid because there are fewer remaining forces.

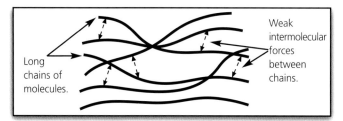

Long chains of molecules.

Weak intermolecular forces between chains.

Thermosets can be softened and moulded into shape the first time they are heated, but they cannot be re-softened and reshaped.

The starting materials first react together when they are heated to form a thermoset, and they release water molecules. This is a condensation reaction. The molecules in the resulting thermoset are crosslinked, which makes the polymer rigid and strong, and unable to be reshaped when reheated.

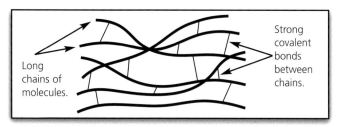

Long chains of molecules.

Strong covalent bonds between chains.

Changing Properties of Plastics

Properties of plastics can be changed to produce a plastic with more desirable properties, by adding chemicals during the initial manufacturing process.

- **Plasticisers** are added to make thermoplastics more flexible. The plasticiser molecules fill the gaps between the chains, allowing them to slip over each other more easily.
- UV (ultraviolet) and thermal **stabilisers** (preservatives) are added to prolong a plastic's life.
- **Crosslinking agents** are added to the thermoplastics to encourage the molecules to form cross links. This increases high-temperature performance (melting point) and gives a more stable form of plastic.

Disposing of Plastics

There are various ways of disposing of plastics. Unfortunately, some of these methods can be harmful to the environment:

Burning
Burning plastics produces air pollution. The carbon dioxide produced contributes to the Greenhouse Effect which results in global warming. Some plastics cannot be burned as they produce toxic fumes, e.g. burning PVC produces hydrogen chloride gas.

Use of Landfill Sites
The problem with most plastics is that they are non-biodegradable. Microorganisms have no effect on them: they will not decompose and rot away. This means that plastic waste builds up.

Synthesis

Oil

Crude Oil

The bar chart below shows the demand for each fraction of crude oil and the relative amounts of each fraction in crude oil.

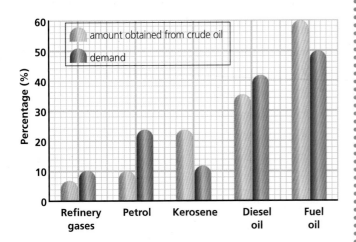

The demand for certain fractions exceeds the supply, especially for shorter-chain hydrocarbons such as refinery gases and petrol. This is because they release energy more quickly by burning and therefore make better fuels.

In order to increase the relative amounts of these fractions, longer-chain hydrocarbons are broken down into shorter-chain hydrocarbons (through cracking – see p.34), some of which have double carbon-carbon bonds.

These compounds are used to fuel transport, to heat homes; to make chemicals for drugs, food, cosmetics and cleaning products; and to make plastics for clothing, bags, electrical equipment etc.

As crude oil runs out, supply decreases, but demand remains the same and so prices increase. Scientists are always trying to find new ways of making the substances that crude oil currently provides.

Vegetable Oils

Vegetable oils are used in cooking and are **unsaturated**. They are liquids at room temperature because they have high levels of **monounsaturated** and **polyunsaturated** fats.

Monounsaturated fats have only one double carbon-carbon bond, for example...

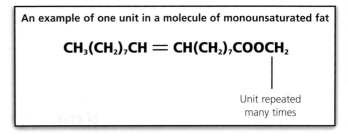

An example of one unit in a molecule of monounsaturated fat

$$CH_3(CH_2)_7CH = CH(CH_2)_7COOCH_2$$

Unit repeated many times

Polyunsaturated fats have two double carbon-carbon bonds, for example...

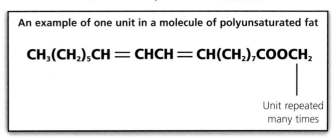

An example of one unit in a molecule of polyunsaturated fat

$$CH_3(CH_2)_5CH = CHCH = CH(CH_2)_7COOCH_2$$

Unit repeated many times

Removing some or all of the double covalent carbon-carbon bonds will raise the melting point of an oil and, therefore, harden it. This can have the advantage of increasing its shelf life, which is an advantage in the food industry.

The oil is hardened by adding hydrogen which breaks the double covalent carbon-carbon bonds. Enough double bonds have to be **hydrogenated** to achieve the right viscosity (thickness). The more hydrogen that is added, the greater the viscosity.

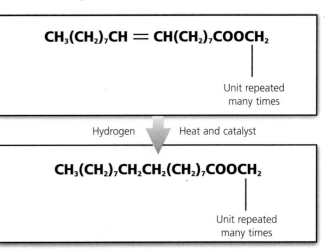

$$CH_3(CH_2)_7CH = CH(CH_2)_7COOCH_2$$

Unit repeated many times

Hydrogen ⟶ Heat and catalyst

$$CH_3(CH_2)_7CH_2CH_2(CH_2)_7COOCH_2$$

Unit repeated many times

Monounsaturated and polyunsaturated oils are far less viscous than saturated oils. This is because they have double covalent carbon-carbon bonds, meaning there are fewer bonds with hydrogen.

Synthesis

Product Development

Synthesis Methods

Chemists can use their knowledge of existing molecules and substances to predict the outcomes of new reactions.

The shape, structure and properties of new products can be predicted using a combination of **computer modelling** and known information. It is even possible to determine how toxic a new substance would be to a human by comparing the developed substance to known compounds using computer modelling.

In any reaction between an acid and a base that we carry out, we can predict the product because we always get a salt and water.

We can see this working when we add the same volumes of hydrochloric acid (HCl, a strong acid) and potassium hydroxide (KOH, a base) together; potassium chloride (KCl) and water are produced (see diagram below).

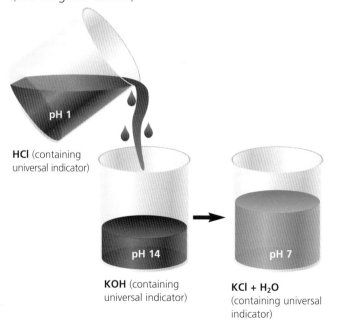

HCl (containing universal indicator)

KOH (containing universal indicator)

KCl + H₂O (containing universal indicator)

Today, developing new substances takes a lot of preparation. To be successful, **synthesis** (the production process) must produce the desired product in a reasonable quantity, quickly and efficiently.

Atom Economy

Scientists make sure the process they use gives high atom economy (see p.39). Reactions with high atom economy are important for sustainable development as they prevent waste. However, not all reactions that give a high yield (output) are the most efficient.

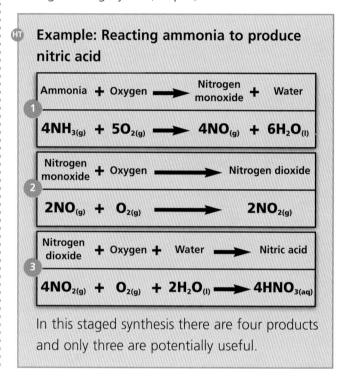

HT **Example: Reacting ammonia to produce nitric acid**

1.

| Ammonia | + | Oxygen | → | Nitrogen monoxide | + | Water |

$$4NH_{3(g)} + 5O_{2(g)} \longrightarrow 4NO_{(g)} + 6H_2O_{(l)}$$

2.

| Nitrogen monoxide | + | Oxygen | → | Nitrogen dioxide |

$$2NO_{(g)} + O_{2(g)} \longrightarrow 2NO_{2(g)}$$

3.

| Nitrogen dioxide | + | Oxygen | + | Water | → | Nitric acid |

$$4NO_{2(g)} + O_{2(g)} + 2H_2O_{(l)} \longrightarrow 4HNO_{3(aq)}$$

In this staged synthesis there are four products and only three are potentially useful.

Drug Synthesis

The development of new medication is a lengthy and expensive process. The drug industry is looking into ways in which timescales and costs can be reduced. Originally, the process involved developing one compound at a time using many steps to produce a successfully trialled drug – this could take up to 20 years.

Today, using computer simulation technology, more compounds can be developed alongside each other. This helps drug companies to select the right target compounds as they compare new structures with known structures and discard those that have been found to be toxic in the past. Only the best compounds are synthesised in the lab to be tested on humans. The most effective compound is then tested on a larger group of volunteers. A third and final **toxicological study** is done on the compound before it goes into production.

Synthesis

Relative Formula Mass, M_r

The **relative formula mass, M_r**, of a compound is the sum of the relative atomic masses of all its elements added together. To calculate M_r, we need to know the formula of the compound, and the relative atomic mass, A_r, of all the atoms involved. The relative atomic mass is the number at the top left of the element symbol:

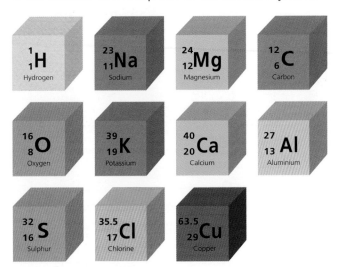

Example 1
Using the data above, calculate the M_r of water, H_2O.

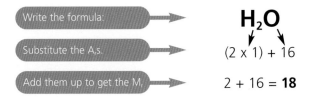

Write the formula: H_2O

Substitute the A_rs. $(2 \times 1) + 16$

Add them up to get the M_r $2 + 16 = \mathbf{18}$

Example 2
Using the data above, calculate the M_r of potassium carbonate, K_2CO_3.

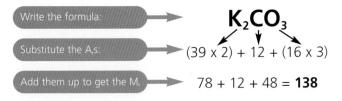

Write the formula: K_2CO_3

Substitute the A_rs: $(39 \times 2) + 12 + (16 \times 3)$

Add them up to get the M_r $78 + 12 + 48 = \mathbf{138}$

Empirical Formula

Empirical formula is the simplest formula which represents the ratio of atoms in a compound. There is one simple rule: **always divide the data you are given by the A_r of the element**. Then simplify the ratio to give you the simplest formula.

Example
Find the empirical formula of an oxide of iron, produced by reacting 1.12g of iron with 0.48g of oxygen. (Relative atomic masses: Fe = 56; O = 16)

> Identify the mass of the elements in the compound…

Masses: Fe = 1.12, O = 0.48

> Divide these masses by their relative atomic masses…

Fe = $\frac{1.12}{56}$ = 0.02   O = $\frac{0.48}{16}$ = 0.03

> Identify the ratio of atoms in the compound and simplify it…

Ratio = $\quad$ x 100 $\Big($ 0.02 : 0.03 $\Big)$ x 100
$\qquad\qquad\qquad\qquad$ 2 : 3

Empirical formula = $\mathbf{Fe_2O_3}$

HT Calculating the Mass of a Product and a Reactant

Sometimes, we need to be able to work out how much of a substance is used up or produced in a chemical reaction.

Example
How much calcium oxide can be produced from 50kg of calcium carbonate? (Relative atomic masses: Ca = 40; C = 12; O = 16).

> Write down the equation:

$$CaCO_3 \rightarrow CaO + CO_2$$

> Work out the M_r of each substance:

$40 + 12 + (3 \times 16) \rightarrow (40 + 16) + [12 + (2 \times 16)]$

> Check the total mass of reactants equals the total mass of the products. If they are not the same, check your work:

$100 \rightarrow 56 + 44$ ✔

> Since the question only mentions calcium oxide and calcium carbonate, you can now ignore the carbon dioxide. You just need the ratio of mass of $CaCO_3$ to mass of CaO.

If 100kg of $CaCO_3$ produces 56kg of CaO, then 1kg of $CaCO_3$ produces $\frac{56}{100}$ kg of CaO, and 50kg of $CaCO_3$ produces $\frac{56}{100}$ x 50 of CaO, = **28kg** of CaO.

Synthesis

Atom Economy

Chemical reactions often produce more than one **product**, and not all of these products are 'useful'. This means that not all of the starting materials (**reactants**) are converted into useful products. **Atom economy** is a measure of the amounts of reactants that end up as useful products.

Calculating Atom Economy

The atom economy of any reaction can be calculated using the following equation:

$$\text{Atom economy} = \frac{\text{Mass of (atoms in) useful product}}{\text{Total mass (of atoms) of product}} \times 100\%$$

Example

How economic is the production of zinc chloride when zinc carbonate is reacted with hydrochloric acid?
(Relative masses: Zn = 65; Cl = 35.5; H = 1; C = 12, O = 16)

First, write down the equation of the reaction:

Zinc carbonate	+	Hydrochloric acid	→	Zinc chloride	+	Water	+	Carbon dioxide

$$ZnCO_{3(s)} + 2HCl_{(aq)} \rightarrow ZnCl_{2(aq)} + H_2O_{(l)} + CO_{2(g)}$$

Mass of atoms in useful product, $ZnCl_2$:

Zn x 1 = 65 x 1 = 65
Cl x 2 = 35.5 x 2 = 71
= **136**

Mass of atoms in waste product, H_2O:

H x 2 = 1 x 2 = 2
O x 1 = 16 x 1 = 16
= **18**

Mass of atoms in waste product, CO_2:

C x 1 = 12 x 1 = 12
O x 2 = 16 x 2 = 32
= **44**

Atom economy $= \dfrac{136}{(136 + 18 + 44)} \times 100$

$= \dfrac{136}{198} \times 100 = \mathbf{68.69\%}$

Calculating Yields

The **expected yield** is the amount of product expected from a reaction, based on the amount of reactants. Companies like to get the highest possible yield from the reaction, for the lowest cost. There are two yields in a reaction:

- **theoretical yield** – calculated from the masses of atoms
- **actual yield** – the actual mass obtained from the reaction.

By comparing these two yields, we can calculate the percentage yield:

$$\text{Percentage yield} = \frac{\text{Actual yield}}{\text{Maximum theoretical yield}} \times 100\%$$

Example

264g of silver chloride was obtained from the reaction of magnesium chloride and silver nitrate.
(Relative atomic masses: Ag = 108; Cl = 35.5)

First, write down the equation of the reaction:

Silver nitrate	+	Magnesium chloride	→	Silver chloride	+	Magnesium nitrate

$$2AgNO_{3(aq)} + MgCl_{2(aq)} \rightarrow 2AgCl_{(s)} + Mg(NO_3)_{2(aq)}$$

Work out the formula mass for AgCl.

Ag x 1 = 108 x 1 = 108
Cl x 1 = 35.5 x 1 = 35.5
= **143.5**

Theoretical yield for AgCl
= 143.5 x 2 = **287g**

2AgCl means there are two lots of AgCl produced

Percentage yield $= \dfrac{\text{Actual yield}}{\text{Theoretical yield}} = \dfrac{264}{287} \times 100$

$= \mathbf{91.9\%}$

Synthesis

Glossary

Addition – when molecules are added together to produce a larger molecule and nothing in the original molecule is left out

Alkane – a saturated hydrocarbon; a molecule with a spine of carbon atoms completely surrounded by hydrogen atoms and held together by single covalent bonds

Alkene – an unsaturated hydrocarbon; a molecule that has a spine of carbon atoms and hydrogen atoms held together by single covalent bonds and at least one double covalent carbon-carbon bond

Condensation – water given off as a by-product of a reaction

Covalent bond – a bond that involves the sharing of one or more pairs of electrons. The atoms combining give the electrons. It generally occurs between non-metal elements

Cracking – a process used to break down long-chain hydrocarbons, generally alkanes, into more useful short-chain hydrocarbons, using high temperatures and a catalyst

Double bond – a covalent bond that involves the sharing of two pairs of electrons

Empirical – the simplest ratio of atoms in a chemical formula

Formula – shows the relative numbers of the different kinds of atoms in a compound

Hydrogenate – to add hydrogen to an unsaturated compound

Monomer – a small molecule which chemically bonds to other monomers to produce a polymer

Monounsaturated – an organic compound that only contains one double covalent carbon-carbon bond

Polymer – a long-chain molecule made up of a large number of monomers that have combined together during polymerisation

Polyunsaturated – an organic compound with more than one double covalent carbon-carbon bond

Saturated hydrocarbon – a molecule that contains only hydrogen and carbon; it has no double covalent carbon-carbon bond so has the maximum possible number of hydrogen atoms

Sustainable development – development that meets the needs of the present without compromising the ability of future generations to meet their own needs

Synthesis – the formation of a compound from its constituent elements

Thermoplastic – a material that will soften when heated and can be moulded into shape. The process of heating and remoulding can be repeated many times

Thermosetting – a material that can be moulded only the first time it is heated. It cannot be softened or remoulded when reheated but it will decompose in extreme heat

Toxicity – an adverse effect of a chemical on a living organism with the severity of toxicity produced being directly proportional to the exposure concentration and time

Unsaturated hydrocarbon – a molecule that contains only hydrogen and carbon; it has at least one double covalent carbon-carbon bond so it has less than the maximum possible number of hydrogen atoms

Unsaturated monomers – small molecules that can join together to form polymers. They contain double or triple carbon bonds and can be saturated by adding hydrogen

---

HT **Expected yield** – the mass of product that is expected from a chemical reaction based on the mass of reactants used

Percentage yield – the mass of product obtained expressed as a percentage of the calculated theoretical yield

Theoretical yield – the mass of product which should be produced if everything goes perfectly; calculated from an equation's relative atomic masses

The Periodic Table and the Elements

All things are made of elements. The known elements are arranged in the periodic table. However, the periodic table is a relatively recent discovery.

* Before we knew about chemical elements, alchemists (early scientists) described things as being made from fire, air, earth and water.
* The idea of elements was first mentioned in the mid-1600s.
* The first modern periodic table had gaps for elements that were yet to be discovered.

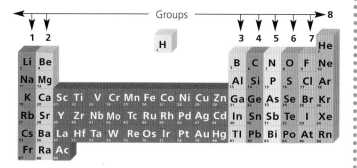

The Atom

Elements are made up of **atoms**. An atom has a nucleus which contains protons and neutrons (the exception is hydrogen which does not contain neutrons). The nucleus is surrounded by orbiting electrons arranged in shells. These particles have different relative masses and charges:

Atomic Particle	Relative Mass	Relative Charge
Proton	1	+1 (positive)
Neutron	1	0 (neutral)
Electron	0 (nearly)	-1 (negative)

An atom has the same number of protons as electrons, so the atom as a whole has no electrical charge.

All the atoms of a particular element have…
* the same number of protons in their nuclei
* the same number of electrons orbiting the nucleus.

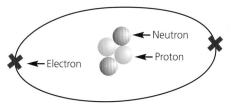

A Representation of a Helium Atom

Atomic Number and Mass Number

All elements in the periodic table have two numbers next to their symbol, for example…

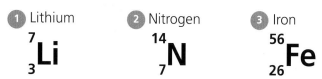

1. Lithium $^{7}_{3}\text{Li}$
2. Nitrogen $^{14}_{7}\text{N}$
3. Iron $^{56}_{26}\text{Fe}$

The number at the bottom is the **atomic number**. This tells us the number of protons (and, therefore, the number of electrons) found in the nucleus of an atom of that element.

The number at the top is the **mass number** (which also doubles up as the relative atomic mass). This tells us the total number of protons and neutrons in the nucleus of an atom of that element.

Element	Atomic Number	Mass Number
Lithium (nucleus contains 3 protons and 4 neutrons)	3	7
Nitrogen (nucleus contains 7 protons and 7 neutrons)	7	14
Iron (nucleus contains 26 protons and 30 neutrons)	26	56

Relative Atomic Mass (A_r)

Atoms are too small for their actual atomic mass to be of much use to us. To make things more manageable we use **relative atomic mass (A_r)**.

Relative atomic mass is the mass of a particular atom compared to the mass of an atom of hydrogen, which is the lightest atom of all. (In fact, we now use $\frac{1}{12}$ the mass of a carbon atom but it does not make a difference.)

In Your Element

Isotopes

The number of **protons** in the atom defines the element. All the atoms of a particular element have the same number of protons in their nuclei; this number is unique to each particular element and is its atomic number.

However, some atoms of the same element can have different numbers of **neutrons**: these are called **isotopes** of the element.

Because isotopes have the same number of protons and the same electron configuration as the element, they have the same chemical properties, so their reactions are the same. They are easy to spot because they have the **same atomic number** but a **different mass number**.

Examples

① Chlorine has two isotopes.

$$^{35}_{17}\text{Cl} \qquad ^{37}_{17}\text{Cl}$$

17 protons   17 protons
17 electrons   17 electrons
18 neutrons   20 neutrons
(35 − 17 = 18)   (37 − 17 = 20)

② Hydrogen has three isotopes.

$$^{1}_{1}\text{H} \qquad ^{2}_{1}\text{H} \qquad ^{3}_{1}\text{H}$$

1 proton   1 proton   1 proton
1 electron   1 electron   1 electron
0 neutrons   1 neutron)   2 neutrons
(1 − 1 = 0)   (2 − 1 = 1)   (3 − 1 = 2)

③ Carbon has three isotopes.

$$^{12}_{6}\text{C} \qquad ^{13}_{6}\text{C} \qquad ^{14}_{6}\text{C}$$

6 protons   6 protons   6 protons
6 electrons   6 electrons   6 electrons
6 neutrons   7 neutrons   8 neutrons
(12 − 6 = 6)   (13 − 6 = 7)   (14 − 6 = 8)

Relative Atomic Mass

The mass numbers in the examples alongside are the atomic masses of each particular isotope of an element. **Relative atomic mass** is an average for the different isotopes of an element.

Chemists use relative atomic masses because they take into account the relative isotopic masses and the abundance of each one.

Example 1: Chlorine

Naturally occurring chlorine consists of about 75% of $^{35}_{17}\text{Cl}$ and 25% of $^{37}_{17}\text{Cl}$, i.e. in a ratio of about 3:1.

So, for every four atoms of chlorine, three of them are $^{35}_{17}\text{Cl}$ and one of them is $^{37}_{17}\text{Cl}$.

So the total atomic mass of these four atoms = (3 x 35) + (1 x 37) = 142

Therefore, the **relative atomic mass** of chlorine is…

$$\frac{142}{4} = 35.5$$

N.B. The relative atomic mass is often not a whole number (as above for chlorine), whereas the relative isotopic masses for an element always are.

Example 2: Magnesium

Magnesium consists of about 80% of $^{24}_{12}\text{Mg}$, 10% of $^{25}_{12}\text{Mg}$ and 10% of $^{26}_{12}\text{Mg}$, i.e. in the ratio of about 8:1:1.

So, for every ten atoms of magnesium, eight of them are $^{24}_{12}\text{Mg}$, one of them is $^{25}_{12}\text{Mg}$ and one of them is $^{26}_{12}\text{Mg}$.

So the total atomic mass of these ten atoms = (8 x 24) + (1 x 25) + (1 x 26) = 243

Therefore, the **relative atomic mass** of magnesium is…

$$\frac{243}{10} = 24.3$$

Electron Configuration

Electron configuration tells us how the electrons are arranged around the nucleus of an atom in energy levels (shells).

- The electrons in an atom occupy the lowest available shells (i.e. the shells nearest to the nucleus).
- The first shell can only contain a maximum of two electrons.
- The shells after the first shell can each hold a maximum of eight electrons.
- We write electron configuration as a series of numbers, for example...

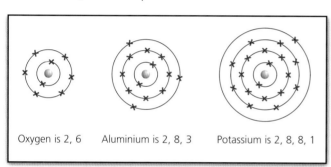

Oxygen is 2, 6   Aluminium is 2, 8, 3   Potassium is 2, 8, 8, 1

Notice that there is a connection between the number of outer electrons and the position of an element in a group: elements in Group 1 have only one electron in their outermost shell, elements in Group 2 have only two electrons in their outermost shell, and so on.

Reactivity of the Elements

How an element reacts depends on...
- the number of electrons in the outermost shell
- the distance the outermost shell is from the influence of the nucleus.

Generally...
- the more electrons there are in the outermost shell and the further they are from the nucleus, the less reactive the element is
- the fewer electrons there are in the outermost shell and the further they are from the nucleus, the more reactive the element is.

Reactivity of Elements in Groups

Group 1: the Alkali Metals
Elements in Group 1 (which all have one electron in their outermost shell) become more reactive as we go down the group. This is because the outermost electron shell gets further away from the influence of the nucleus, meaning the electron is more easily lost.

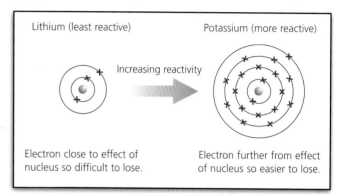

Lithium (least reactive) — Increasing reactivity — Potassium (more reactive)

Electron close to effect of nucleus so difficult to lose.   Electron further from effect of nucleus so easier to lose.

Group 7: the Halogens
Elements in Group 7 (which all have seven electrons in their outermost shell) become less reactive as we go down the group. This is because the outermost electron shell gets further away from the influence of the nucleus, meaning an electron is less easily gained.

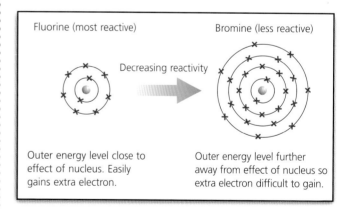

Fluorine (most reactive) — Decreasing reactivity — Bromine (less reactive)

Outer energy level close to effect of nucleus. Easily gains extra electron.   Outer energy level further away from effect of nucleus so extra electron difficult to gain.

Group 8 / 0: the Noble Gases
Elements in Group 8 (Group 0) all have full outermost electron shells. This means that they do not need to lose or gain electrons in reactions in order to become stable, and so they do not react with many other elements.

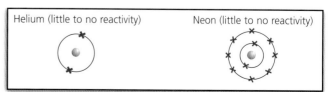

Helium (little to no reactivity)   Neon (little to no reactivity)

In Your Element

The Modern Periodic Table – Electronic Configuration of the First 20 Elements

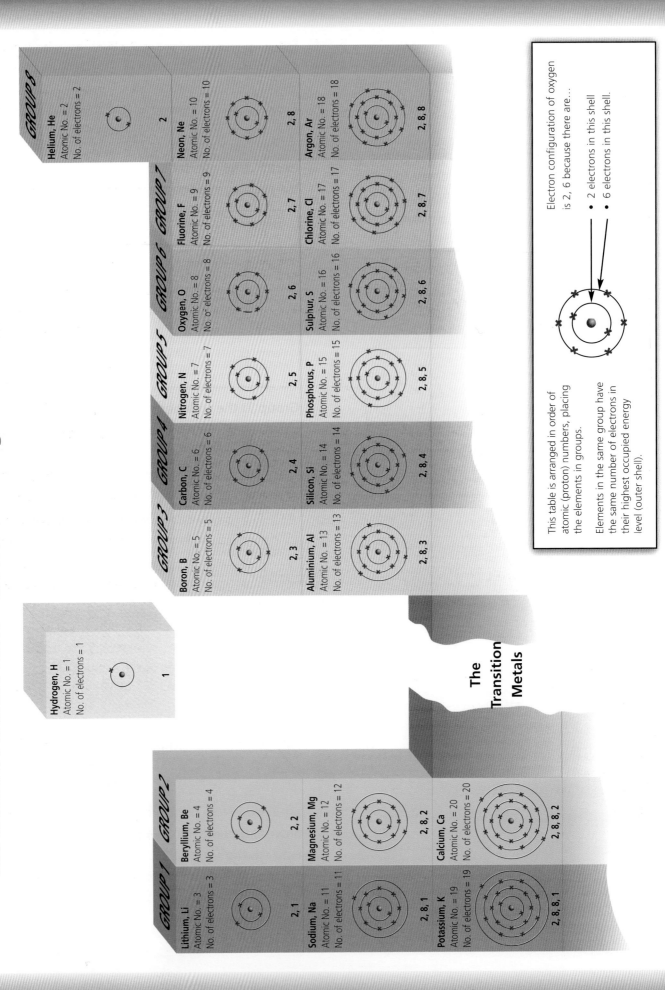

Hydrogen, H
Atomic No. = 1
No. of electrons = 1

1

GROUP1

Lithium, Li
Atomic No. = 3
No. of electrons = 3

2, 1

Sodium, Na
Atomic No. = 11
No. of electrons = 11

2, 8, 1

Potassium, K
Atomic No. = 19
No. of electrons = 19

2, 8, 8, 1

GROUP2

Beryllium, Be
Atomic No. = 4
No. of electrons = 4

2, 2

Magnesium, Mg
Atomic No. = 12
No. of electrons = 12

2, 8, 2

Calcium, Ca
Atomic No. = 20
No. of electrons = 20

2, 8, 8, 2

GROUP3

Boron, B
Atomic No. = 5
No. of electrons = 5

2, 3

Aluminium, Al
Atomic No. = 13
No. of electrons = 13

2, 8, 3

GROUP4

Carbon, C
Atomic No. = 6
No. of electrons = 6

2, 4

Silicon, Si
Atomic No. = 14
No. of electrons = 14

2, 8, 4

GROUP5

Nitrogen, N
Atomic No. = 7
No. of electrons = 7

2, 5

Phosphorus, P
Atomic No. = 15
No. of electrons = 15

2, 8, 5

GROUP6

Oxygen, O
Atomic No. = 8
No. of electrons = 8

2, 6

Sulphur, S
Atomic No. = 16
No. of electrons = 16

2, 8, 6

GROUP7

Fluorine, F
Atomic No. = 9
No. of electrons = 9

2, 7

Chlorine, Cl
Atomic No. = 17
No. of electrons = 17

2, 8, 7

GROUP8

Helium, He
Atomic No. = 2
No. of electrons = 2

2

Neon, Ne
Atomic No. = 10
No. of electrons = 10

2, 8

Argon, Ar
Atomic No. = 18
No. of electrons = 18

2, 8, 8

The Transition Metals

Electron configuration of oxygen is 2, 6 because there are...
- 2 electrons in this shell.
- 6 electrons in this shell.

This table is arranged in order of atomic (proton) numbers, placing the elements in groups.

Elements in the same group have the same number of electrons in their highest occupied energy level (outer shell).

44

Ionic Bonding

To become chemically stable, atoms lose or gain electrons in order to fill their outermost energy level (shell). These electrons must be accepted by, or donated by, other atoms. Sometimes electrons are completely transferred. This results in the formation of an **ionic bond**.

An ionic bond occurs between a **metal atom** and a **non-metal atom** and involves a transfer of electrons from one atom to the other in order to form electrically charged 'atoms' called **ions** which may be positively or negatively charged. Each ion has a complete outermost electron shell, just like the very unreactive noble gases.

Example 1

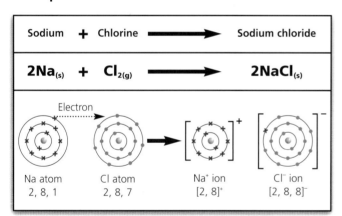

The sodium atom has 1 electron in its outer shell which is transferred to the chlorine atom. Both now have 8 electrons in their outer shell (i.e. complete outer shells). The atoms are now ions: Na^+ and Cl^-. The compound formed is sodium chloride, $NaCl$.

Example 2

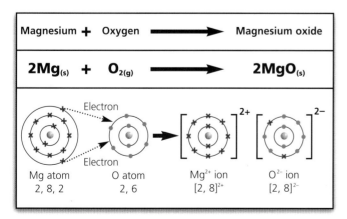

The magnesium atom has 2 electrons in its outer shell which are transferred to the oxygen atom. Both have 8 electrons in their outer shell. The atoms are now ions: Mg^{2+} and O^{2-}. The compound formed is magnesium oxide, MgO.

Example 3

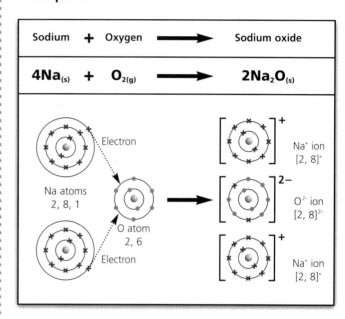

The sodium atom has 1 electron in its outer shell, which is transferred to the oxygen atom. Sodium has 8 electrons in its outermost shell but oxygen still only has 7, so it needs another. Another sodium atom, which has 1 electron in its outer shell, transfers an electron to the oxygen atom. Both sodium atoms and the oxygen atom now have 8 electrons in their outermost shell. The atoms are now ions: Na^+ and O^{2-}. The compound formed is sodium oxide, Na_2O.

Predicting Formulae

Ionic compounds are neutral because the charges on the ions cancel each other out. Knowing this and the charge on the ions, we can predict formulae for any ionic compound (see p.62).

Example: Predicting the Formula for Magnesium Chloride

Magnesium ions have a 2+ charge, Mg^{2+}. Chlorine ions have a 1– charge, Cl^-.

The charge on two chlorine ions balances out the charge on the magnesium ion: $Mg^{2+} + 2 \times Cl^- = MgCl_2$.

In Your Element

Ionic Structures and Electrolysis

Properties of Ionic Compounds

Ionic compounds, e.g. sodium chloride, consist of a giant lattice held together by the forces of attraction between the positive (sodium) ions, **cations**, and the negative (chloride) ions, **anions**.

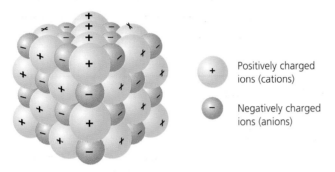

Positively charged ions (cations)

Negatively charged ions (anions)

Magnesium oxide consists of a similar giant lattice made up of Mg^{2+} and O^{2-} ions.

Both of these examples are **binary salts** (salts which are made of anions and cations).

Ionic compounds...

- have high melting and boiling points due to the strong electrostatic forces of attraction which hold them together
- conduct electricity when molten or in solution because the charged ions are free to move about
- often (but not always) dissolve in water. When they do dissolve, strong forces of attraction are formed between the ions and the water
- are crystalline due to the regular arrangement of their ions.

N.B. Sodium chloride dissolves in water. Magnesium oxide is insoluble.

Electrolysis

When a direct current is passed through a liquid containing ions, the ions move to the electrode of opposite charge.

The ions which are positively charged (cations) move towards the **negative cathode.**

The ions which are negatively charged (anions) move towards the **positive anode**.

When the ions get to the electrodes, they are **discharged** (lose their charges). The negative ions lose electrons to the anode. The positive ions gain electrons from the cathode. During discharge, atoms of elements are formed.

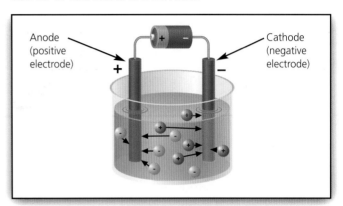

Anode (positive electrode)

Cathode (negative electrode)

When copper is needed in a pure form, e.g. for electrical circuits, it is purified by electrolysis:

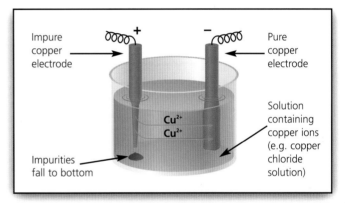

Impure copper electrode

Pure copper electrode

Solution containing copper ions (e.g. copper chloride solution)

Cu^{2+}
Cu^{2+}

Impurities fall to bottom

HT The reactions at the electrodes can be written as half equations. This means that we write separate equations for what is happening at each of the electrodes during electrolysis.

At the positive anode:

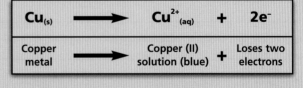

$Cu_{(s)}$	$\longrightarrow$	$Cu^{2+}_{(aq)}$	+	$2e^-$
Copper metal	$\longrightarrow$	Copper (II) solution (blue)	+	Loses two electrons

At the negative cathode:

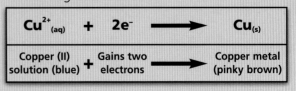

$Cu^{2+}_{(aq)}$	+	$2e^-$	$\longrightarrow$	$Cu_{(s)}$
Copper (II) solution (blue)	+	Gains two electrons	$\longrightarrow$	Copper metal (pinky brown)

In Your Element

Electrolysis of Molten Aluminium Oxide

Molten aluminium oxide is a molten binary salt. It can be electrolysed to produce aluminium. During this process...

Aluminium oxide	$\longrightarrow$	Aluminium	+	Oxygen
$2Al_2O_{3(l)}$	$\longrightarrow$	$4Al_{(l)}$	+	$3O_{2(g)}$

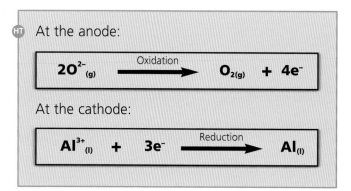

HT At the anode:

$$2O^{2-}_{(g)} \xrightarrow{\text{Oxidation}} O_{2(g)} + 4e^-$$

At the cathode:

$$Al^{3+}_{(l)} + 3e^- \xrightarrow{\text{Reduction}} Al_{(l)}$$

Pure Metals

A pure metal contains only atoms of that element. Most metals extracted from the ground need to be purified. When they have been purified they will show many of the following general properties:

Properties of Pure Metals

- Good conductivity (they are good conductors of heat and electricity).
- Dense (feel heavy).
- Malleable (can be hammered into shape without cracking).
- Soft in comparison to their alloys.
- Can be magnetic, e.g. iron, cobalt and nickel.
- Shiny when polished.
- High melting and boiling points.
- Strong under tension and compression.
- Sonorous (will ring when hit).
- Ductile (can be drawn into a wire).

Alloys

Many metals are far more useful when they are **not pure**. Mixing other substances such as another metal, carbon or silicon can change the properties of any metal.

The substances used are dissolved into the molten main metal. The resulting **alloy** has a greater range of uses than the main metal. Remember, an alloy is a **mixture**.

An alloy can have…

- a lower melting point (useful for solder)
- increased corrosion resistance (useful for anything that will be exposed to air and water)
- increased chemical resistance (useful for storing chemicals)
- increased strength and hardness (useful in construction of bridges, aircraft, cars etc.).

Examples of Using an Alloy

Pure iron is not good for building things because it is too soft and stretches easily. It also corrodes easily. If a small amount of carbon is added to iron, mild steel is produced which is hard and strong, so it can be used for building things.

If nickel and chromium are mixed with iron, stainless steel is produced which is hard and rustproof, so can be used in areas that are exposed to air and water, e.g. cutlery.

In Your Element

Glossary

Alloy – a metal made by mixing a metal with another metal or substance; the alloy has different properties from the pure metal

Atomic number – the number of protons in the nucleus of an atom; it is also the number of electrons orbiting the nucleus

Binary salt – a simple salt that is made of a cation and an anion, e.g. sodium chloride, NaCl

Conductivity – the ability of a substance to conduct electrical current (and heat)

Electrode – the conducting rod or plate that carries electricity in and out of a molten or aqueous solution of salt during electrolysis

Electrolysis – the splitting up of a molten or aqueous solution of salt by passing a direct electrical current through a liquid containing ions

Electronic configuration – the arrangement of electrons around the nucleus of an element. It can be represented by diagrams or numbers and always starts with the inner shell, e.g. lithium (2, 1)

Electron – a particle which carries a negative charge; arranged in shells (or energy levels) around the nucleus of an atom

Formula – shows the relative numbers of atoms of different elements in a compound

Ion – a positively or negatively charged particle formed when an atom (or group of atoms) loses or gains electrons

Ionic bonding – a type of bonding that involves the transfer of one or more electrons from a metal atom to a non-metal atom. During this process, ions are formed. The atoms that lose electrons become positively charged because they have more (positively charged) protons than electrons. The atoms that gain electrons become negatively charged because they have more (negatively charged) electrons than protons

Isotopes – atoms of the same element with the same atomic number but different mass numbers, because they have different numbers of neutrons, e.g. $^{12}_{6}C$ (carbon-12) and $^{14}_{6}C$ (carbon-14)

Malleability – the ability of a metal to be hammered into different shapes without cracking or breaking

Mass number – the total number of protons and neutrons in the nucleus of an atom

Neutron – an atomic particle found in the nucleus of an atom; it has a similar mass to a proton but it does not have a charge

Nucleus – the central part of an atom made up of small particles called protons and neutrons

Periodic table – a list of all the different kinds of elements, arranged into a pattern according to the structure of the elements' atoms and the way in which they behave

Proton – an atomic particle found in the nucleus of an atom; it has a similar mass to a neutron but it has a positive charge

Relative atomic mass – the average mass of an element's isotopes compared with the atom of $^{12}_{6}C$ (carbon-12)

Relative isotopic mass – the mass of a particular isotope of an element compared with the atom of $^{12}_{6}C$ (carbon-12)

The Covalent Bond

A **covalent bond** occurs between non-metal atoms and forms a very strong bond in which electrons are shared. Atoms need to share electrons so they can fill their outer shells. A covalent bond can occur between atoms of the same element or atoms of different elements. It results in the formation of **molecules**.

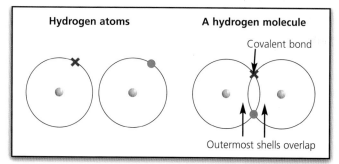

A **single covalent bond** is formed when two atoms share one pair of electrons. Each atom shares one electron in the bond, as in the example above – a hydrogen molecule.

If two pairs of electrons are shared, a **double covalent bond** is formed. Each atom shares two of its electrons in the bond.

If three pairs of electrons are shared, a **triple covalent bond** is formed. Each atom shares three of its electrons in the bond.

Examples

Chlorine atoms join together to form diatomic chlorine molecules (Cl$_2$).

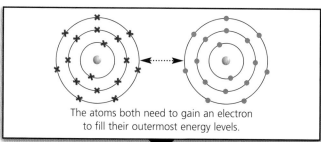

The atoms both need to gain an electron to fill their outermost energy levels.

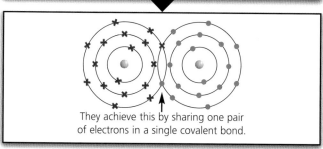

They achieve this by sharing one pair of electrons in a single covalent bond.

Oxygen atoms join together to form diatomic oxygen molecules (O$_2$).

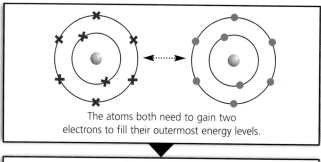

The atoms both need to gain two electrons to fill their outermost energy levels.

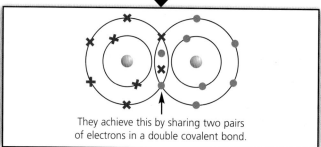

They achieve this by sharing two pairs of electrons in a double covalent bond.

Nitrogen atoms join together to form nitrogen molecules (N$_2$).

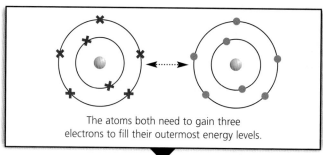

The atoms both need to gain three electrons to fill their outermost energy levels.

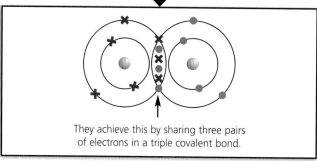

They achieve this by sharing three pairs of electrons in a triple covalent bond.

HT ## Examples of Covalent Compounds

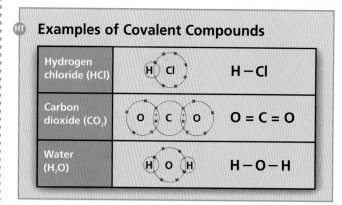

Hydrogen chloride (HCl)	H Cl	H – Cl
Carbon dioxide (CO$_2$)	O C O	O = C = O
Water (H$_2$O)	H O H	H – O – H

Chemical Structures

Covalent Structures – Simple Molecules

Simple covalent structures are molecules with relatively few atoms. There are strong forces between the atoms in the molecules, but there are weak forces between the molecules (weak inter-molecular forces).

This means that simple molecules have low melting and boiling points and have no overall charge so they cannot conduct electricity. They do not attract water molecules so they often do not dissolve in water. Covalent molecules can dissolve in non-aqueous solutions (i.e. a substance that is liquid or molten and does not contain water).

At room temperature many substances exist as gases, usually made up of molecules consisting of more than one atom. Again, there are strong covalent bonds within them but virtually no force of attraction between them. For example…

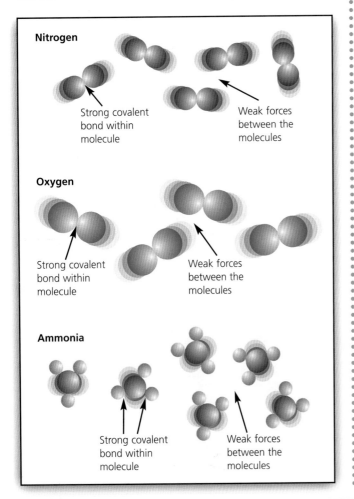

Nitrogen

Strong covalent bond within molecule

Weak forces between the molecules

Oxygen

Strong covalent bond within molecule

Weak forces between the molecules

Ammonia

Strong covalent bond within molecule

Weak forces between the molecules

The Halogens

The most common elements of Group 7 are chlorine, bromine and iodine. They are **diatomic molecules** (molecules containing two atoms which are covalently bonded by a pair of electrons). They cannot occur as single atoms.

They can be solid, liquid or gas at room temperature depending on the strength of the forces holding the molecules together.

Chlorine
The attraction between chlorine molecules is weak so the melting and boiling points are low. Chlorine is a gas at room temperature.

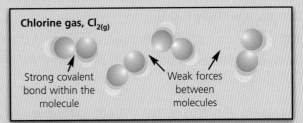

Chlorine gas, $Cl_{2(g)}$

Strong covalent bond within the molecule

Weak forces between molecules

Bromine
The attraction between the molecules is slightly stronger than chlorine, but they are still weak. Bromine's melting and boiling points are still low, but it is a liquid at room temperature.

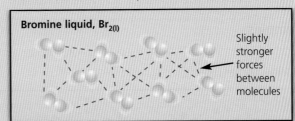

Bromine liquid, $Br_{2(l)}$

Slightly stronger forces between molecules

Iodine
The inter-molecular forces are stronger still. The molecules do not come apart from each other easily. In fact, iodine boils at 184°C but the covalent bonds within the molecules do not break.

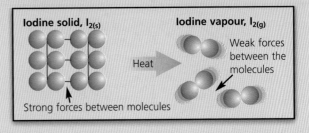

Iodine solid, $I_{2(s)}$

Iodine vapour, $I_{2(g)}$

Heat

Weak forces between the molecules

Strong forces between molecules

Covalent Structures – Giant Molecules

Giant covalent structures may have many atoms joined to each other covalently throughout the whole molecule. This makes their properties very different from those of simple covalently bonded molecules.

Each carbon atom in the structures of diamond and graphite shares its electrons with the atom next to it so that they all have a complete outermost shell.

Diamond (A Form of Carbon)

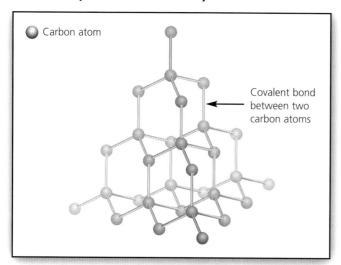

Carbon atom

Covalent bond between two carbon atoms

Diamond is a giant, rigid, covalent structure (lattice) where each carbon atom forms **four covalent bonds** with other carbon atoms. The large number of covalent bonds results in diamond having very high melting and boiling points, which makes the diamond very hard but unable to conduct electricity.

Graphite (A Form of Carbon)

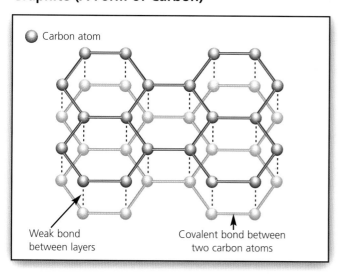

Carbon atom

Weak bond between layers

Covalent bond between two carbon atoms

Graphite is a giant, covalent structure (lattice) in which each carbon atom forms **three covalent bonds** with other carbon atoms in a layered structure. The layers can slide past each other, making it soft and slippery. Like diamond, graphite has a high melting point and a high boiling point. There are weak forces of attraction between layers, so one electron from each carbon atom can be delocalised (moved), which allows graphite to conduct heat and electricity.

Bonding in Metals

Metal atoms form giant crystalline structures. The atoms are packed tightly together so the outer electrons get separated from the atom. The result is a lattice structure of positive ions in a sea of free electrons.

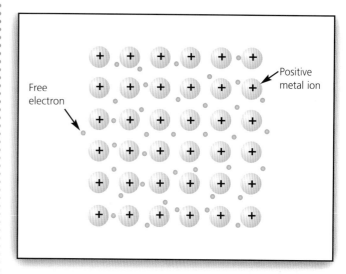

Free electron

Positive metal ion

Metals are very good conductors of electricity because their electrons can move freely within the structure, carrying the electric charge.

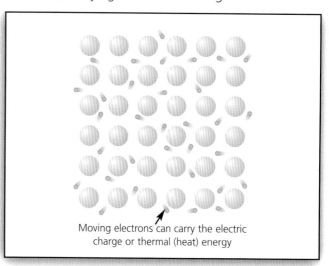

Moving electrons can carry the electric charge or thermal (heat) energy

Chemical Structures

Other Carbon Structures

A third form of carbon (other than diamond and graphite) was discovered in 1985. Scientists fired lasers at graphite carbon clusters to see what would happen and, by chance, different forms of carbon were found. They repeated the experiment and found that the same thing happened each time. The most stable and most common form was carbon-60. Scientists were excited by the discovery, but no use for the carbon had been found.

Buckminster Fullerenes

Carbon-60 became known as Buckminster fullerenes (or 'buckyballs'). Fullerenes are closed carbon cages found in common soot. The carbon-60 was isolated and synthesised and its structure was examined. The following properties were found:

- It was a closed carbon structure with unsaturated carbon-carbon bonding, both double and single.
- It behaved unusually and showed excellent stability – stronger than diamond.
- It could bounce and return to its original shape.
- It could spin at high speeds.
- It was not very reactive but it was the only form of carbon that could be dissolved.
- It was 1 nanometre in diameter (1nm); this was an early milestone in nanotechnology research.

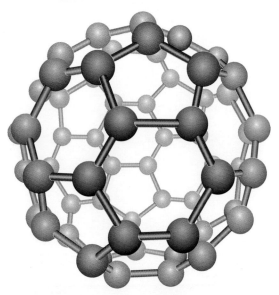

Carbon-60: Buckminster Fullerene

Carbon Nanotubes

Another different form of carbon was developed in 1991 from half an atom of Buckminster fullerene (i.e. half a 'buckyball'). It looks like a single layer of graphite made into a tube. It was found to be the strongest form of carbon.

Carbon nanotubes (CNTs) are flexible and are able to bend up or down to contact an electrode.

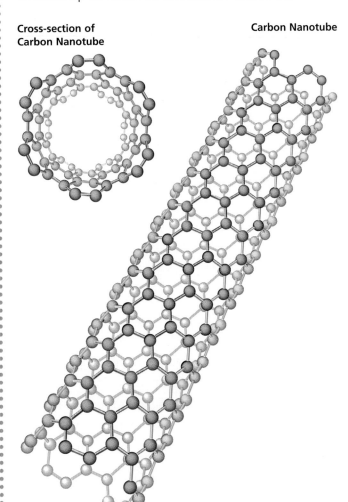

Cross-section of Carbon Nanotube

Carbon Nanotube

Uses of Carbon Structures

Scientists have proposed a variety of uses for carbon fullerenes and nanotubes such as...

- superconductors for use in conducting electricity because they have no electrical resistance
- transistors and diodes (in circuits)
- ion storage for batteries
- reinforcement in buildings etc. because they are very flexible
- industrial catalysts.

Chemical Structures

Representing Molecular Structures

All molecules have a structure. The structure can be simple or complex. Molecular structures can be represented in either two dimensions (2-D) or three dimensions (3-D).

Structure of Sodium Chloride

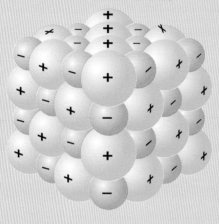

2-D Models

It is easy to draw a representation of molecular structures. Drawing 2-D models is good for representing small molecules and atoms. For example...

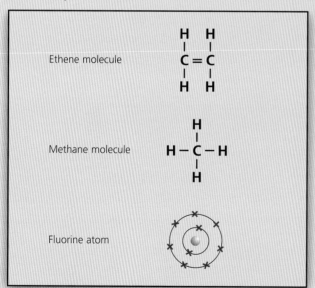

Ethene molecule

Methane molecule

Fluorine atom

However, it is hard to see...

- how atoms are arranged within the structure of the molecule
- how electrons are arranged in an atom (to help explain chemical reactions).

3-D Models

3-D models can either be 'stick and ball models' or computer simulations. Using computer simulation means that the models can be moved and viewed from different angles. For example...

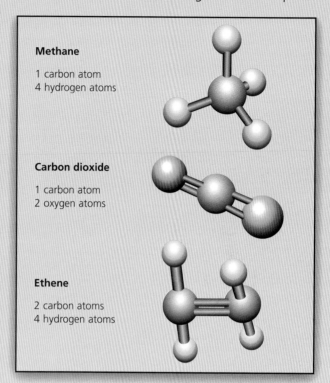

Methane

1 carbon atom
4 hydrogen atoms

Carbon dioxide

1 carbon atom
2 oxygen atoms

Ethene

2 carbon atoms
4 hydrogen atoms

Computer simulations can show how adding individual atoms to the structure can change the shape of the molecule.

3-D models can also show how the electrons are arranged and how they move around the nucleus of an atom. For example...

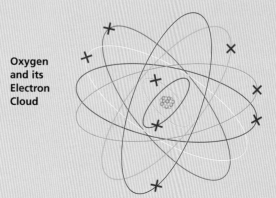

Oxygen and its Electron Cloud

Computer simulations enable us to study the geometry and properties of molecules. We can view the structure and composition of molecules.

Chemical Structures

Chemical-based Therapy

Chemical-based therapy refers to any form of medication that is taken to alleviate (relieve) symptoms of an illness or ailment. It ranges from prescribed medicines to homeopathic treatments. All compounds that exist are chemicals.

> **HT** Many chemical-based therapies are effective, for example:
>
> - **Chemotherapy** is a drug treatment widely used in the treatment of cancer. It is used to try to kill cancer cells and to stop the spreading of the cancer. It is very effective.
>
> - **Antibiotics** are drugs used to destroy bacteria which cause infections and illnesses such as tuberculosis, cholera and tetanus. They have been used successfully for years.

How Medicines Work

Most medicines are designed to replace substances that are deficient or missing in the body. Some medicines can alter the activity of the cells. They can also destroy infectious microorganisms or abnormal cells.

Homeopathic Medicine

Some medicines that alter the activity of the cells are **homeopathic treatments**. They use very weak, diluted doses of compounds or drugs that, if strong enough, would cause symptoms of the illness in a healthy person. The word homeopathy comes from Greek words meaning 'similar suffering'.

Homeopathic medicine works on the 'like for like' principle, i.e. by putting a tiny dose of drugs (which would cause symptoms of an illness) in the person, this causes the body to kickstart the natural healing process.

Each homeopathic medicine is tailored to the individual patient, not purely to the general symptoms.

Example

A homeopathic treatment for hay fever uses *allium cepa* made from an extract of onion. Onion makes the eyes sting and the nose run etc. This makes the body begin to treat such symptoms naturally.

Arguments Against Homeopathy

Established scientific theory uses the way of opposites: illness and disease must be fought off naturally or by taking man-made medicines to dispel the symptoms of that illness / disease from the body.

Homeopathy goes against established scientific theory, using the way of 'similars': treating illness and disease by taking small doses that will bring on symptoms of that illness or disease.

Studies and research have been carried out into the effectiveness of homeopathic treatments, but no conclusive evidence has been obtained: whilst many people claim the treatments work for them, others do not detect any change in their health.

Some scientists believe that homeopathic treatments simply have a **placebo effect**, i.e. people *believe* they experience relief following the administration of an unreactive medicine / substance. Homeopathic medicines are inert (unreactive) substances (e.g. sugar) which have a very temporary effect on the patient.

The general consensus from scientists is that the laws of physics and chemistry would need to be rewritten in order to make sense of how homeopathy works.

Glossary

Buckminster fullerenes (buckyballs, carbon-60) – a form of carbon that has molecules made of 60 carbon atoms. The atoms fold around and join together to make a ball shape. The carbon atoms form shapes of pentagons and hexagons like a football

Carbon nanotube – a form of carbon made from a single layer of graphite (a grapheme), rolled up to make a tube

Conductivity – a substance's ability to conduct electrical current (and heat)

Covalent bond – a bond between two atoms in which both atoms share one or more electron(s)

Diamond – a substance made of carbon that has a giant molecular structure. Each carbon atom is held to the four carbon atoms around it by very strong covalent bonds

Giant covalent structure – a crystalline structure in which all of the atoms are linked together by a network of bonds extending throughout the crystal, e.g. diamond, graphite

Graphite – a substance made of carbon that has a giant molecular structure. Each carbon atom is bonded to three other carbon atoms by strong covalent bonds, forming a sheet of carbon atoms. Many of these sheets are layered together and held in place by weak covalent bonds

Halogens – non-metals found in Group 7 of the periodic table. They exist as diatomic molecules and are known as the 'salt-formers'

Homeopathic – a holistic medicine used to treat the whole state (mind and body); based on the principle of treating like with like. It uses extreme dilutions of animal, vegetable or mineral preparations to stimulate the human body's innate healing system

Inter-molecular force – found in simple molecular solids and liquids such as water, it is the weak force of attraction that holds the molecules together. These forces can easily be overcome by heating the substance

Simple molecular structure – atoms in the molecules are held together with strong covalent bonds; the molecules are held together within their structure by weak inter-molecular bonds. They have low melting and boiling points

How Fast? How Furious?

Rates of Reaction

Rates of chemical reactions can be increased so that the reactions take place more quickly. This can be achieved by...

- increasing the **temperature** of the reaction
- increasing the **surface area** of the solid reactant
- increasing the **concentration** of one of the reactants.

The results of many rates-of-reaction experiments can be recorded accurately using appropriate **data-logging equipment**.

Collision Theory

Chemical reactions only occur when reacting particles collide with each other with sufficient energy to react.

The minimum amount of energy required to cause this reaction is called the **activation energy**. Increasing the frequency and energy of collisions increases the rate of the reaction.

Changing the Rates of Reactions

Low Temperature	High Temperature
In a cold reaction mixture the particles are moving quite slowly – the particles collide with each other less often, with less energy, and fewer collisions are successful. 	If we heat the reaction mixture, the particles move more quickly – the particles collide with each other more often, with greater energy, and many more collisions are successful. 
Small Surface Area	**Large Surface Area**
Large particles have a small surface area in relation to their volume – fewer particles are exposed and available for collisions. This results in fewer collisions and a slower reaction. 	Small particles have a large surface area in relation to their volume – more particles are exposed and available for collisions. This results in more collisions and a faster reaction. 
Low Concentration	**High Concentration**
In a reaction where one or both reactants are in low concentrations, the particles are spread out and collide with each other less often, resulting in fewer successful collisions. 	In a reaction where one or both reactants are in high concentrations, the particles are packed close together and collide with each other more often, resulting in more successful collisions. 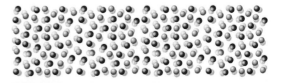

Examples of Changing Rates of Reactions

Calcium carbonate reacts with hydrochloric acid to produce calcium chloride.

Calcium carbonate	+	Hydrochloric acid	→	Calcium chloride	+ Water +	Carbon dioxide

$$CaCO_{3(s)} + 2HCl_{(aq)} \rightarrow CaCl_{2(aq)} + H_2O_{(l)} + CO_{2(g)}$$

We can measure how long it takes for the calcium carbonate to react completely (by disappearing in the acid) and see how changing factors can affect the rate of the reaction.

1 Heating the solution makes the reaction occur more quickly.

2 Increasing the concentration of the acid makes the reaction occur more quickly.

3 Making the solid have a larger surface area increases the rate of the reaction. This can be seen by measuring the amount of carbon dioxide given off every minute. Calcium carbonate chips and then an equal mass of finely crushed calcium carbonate can be used.

N.B. There is the same mass of calcium carbonate in both reactions, so the same volume of CO₂ is produced.

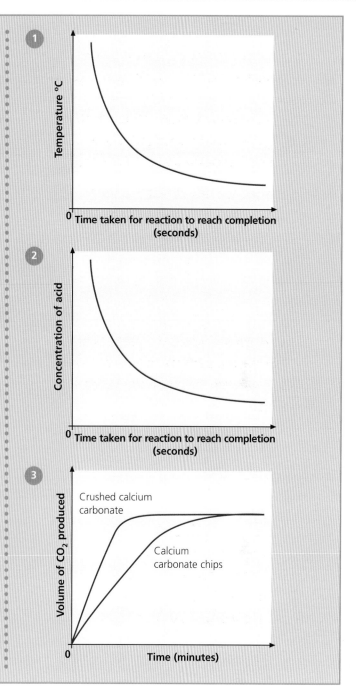

Catalysts

A **catalyst** is a substance which increases the rate of a chemical reaction, without being used up in the process. Catalysts are specific: different reactions require different catalysts. Because catalysts are not used up, only small amounts of them are needed.

Catalysts work by reducing the activation energy (i.e. the minimum energy) needed for a reaction to happen.

Since catalysts lower the amount of energy needed for successful collisions, more collisions will be successful and the reaction will be faster. Also, they provide a surface for the molecules to attach to, thereby increasing the chances of molecules bumping into each other.

How Fast? How Furious?

Catalysts (cont.)

Consider the decomposition (breaking down) of hydrogen peroxide:

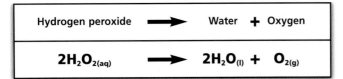

Hydrogen peroxide $\longrightarrow$ Water **+** Oxygen
$2H_2O_{2(aq)} \longrightarrow 2H_2O_{(l)} + O_{2(g)}$

We can measure the rate of this reaction by measuring the amount of oxygen given off at one minute intervals. This reaction happens very slowly, unless we add a catalyst of manganese (IV) oxide. With the catalyst, plenty of fizzing can be seen as the oxygen is given off.

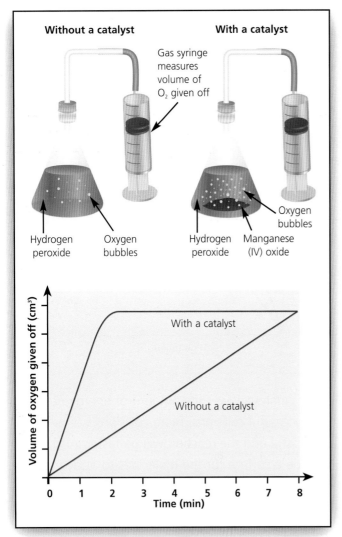

N.B. *If the same amount of hydrogen peroxide is used in both demonstrations then the same volume of oxygen is given off in total. It just takes different amounts of time.*

Catalysts are used a lot in industrial processes to speed up reactions and make production more economical, for example…
- the cracking of hydrocarbons uses broken pottery
- the manufacture of ammonia uses iron.

Enzymes

An enzyme is a **biological catalyst**. Enzymes control the rate of chemical reactions which occur in living organisms. The reactions take place in cells. If enzymes were not used to increase the rate of biochemical reactions (chemical reactions that happen in the body), these reactions would be so slow that life would not exist.

Enzymes work best under certain conditions of temperature and pH, for example…
- the enzyme amylase, found in human saliva, works best at a pH of about 7.3
- the enzyme protease, found in the human stomach, needs to be in very acidic conditions to work well.

Different enzymes have different optimum temperatures. The enzymes in human bodies work best at about 37°C.

Enzymes are protein molecules with high specificity whose molecules have been assembled into particular shapes allowing reactants to be broken down:

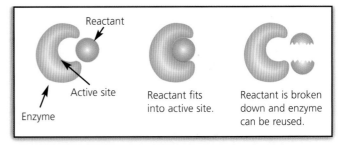

If a protein molecule is denatured by extreme temperature or extreme pH, its shape is changed irreversibly and the reactant no longer fits into the active site, meaning it cannot be broken down.

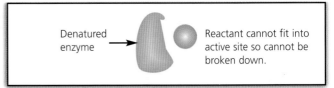

How Fast? How Furious?

Temperature Changes in Reactions

Many chemical reactions are accompanied by a temperature change.

Exothermic reactions are accompanied by a rise in temperature. Thermal (heat) energy is transferred out to the surroundings. Combustion is an example of an exothermic reaction:

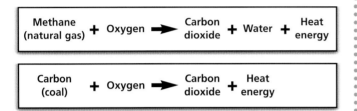

Other exothermic reactions include…
• respiration in body cells
• hydrolysation of ethene to form ethanol
• neutralising alkalis with acids.

Endothermic reactions are accompanied by a fall in temperature. Thermal energy is transferred in from the surroundings. Dissolving ammonium nitrate crystals in water is an example of an endothermic reaction:

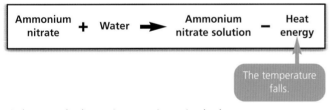

The temperature falls.

Other endothermic reactions include...
• the reaction between citric acid and sodium hydrogen carbonate solution
• polymerisation of ethene to polyethene (see p.34)
• reduction of silver ions to silver in photography.

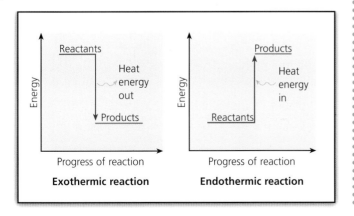

Making and Breaking Bonds

Energy must be supplied to break chemical bonds.

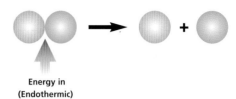

Energy in (Endothermic)

Energy is released when chemical bonds are made.

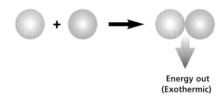

Energy out (Exothermic)

In order to produce new substances in a chemical reaction, the bonds in the reactants must be broken and new bonds must be made in the products. For example…

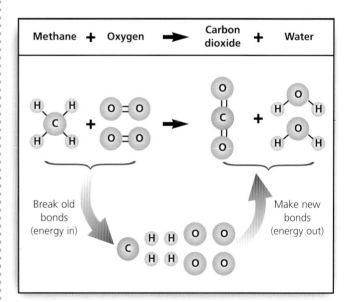

If more energy is needed to break old bonds than is released when new bonds are made, the reaction is endothermic overall.

If more energy is released when new bonds are made than is needed to break the old bonds, the reaction is exothermic overall.

How Fast? How Furious?

Reversible Reactions

Some chemical reactions are **reversible**. This means that the products will react to give the reactants that we started with.

$$A + B \rightleftharpoons C + D$$

A and B react to produce C and D, but also C and D can react to produce A and B.

Example 1

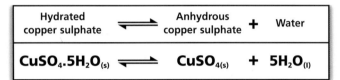

| Hydrated copper sulphate | $\rightleftharpoons$ | Anhydrous copper sulphate | + | Water |

$$CuSO_4.5H_2O_{(s)} \rightleftharpoons CuSO_{4(s)} + 5H_2O_{(l)}$$

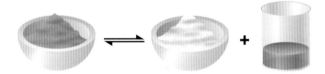

Blue crystals of hydrated copper sulphate become white anhydrous copper sulphate on heating, as water is removed.

Example 2

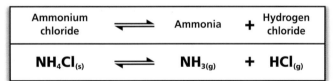

| Ammonium chloride | $\rightleftharpoons$ | Ammonia | + | Hydrogen chloride |

$$NH_4Cl_{(s)} \rightleftharpoons NH_{3(g)} + HCl_{(g)}$$

Solid ammonium chloride decomposes when heated to produce ammonia and hydrogen chloride gas, both of which are colourless.

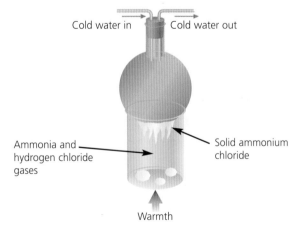

Cold water in — Cold water out

Ammonia and hydrogen chloride gases — Solid ammonium chloride

Warmth

Ammonia reacts with hydrogen chloride gas to produce clouds of white ammonium chloride powder.

Reactions in Equilibrium

When a reversible reaction occurs in a closed system (where no reactants are added and no products are removed) then an **equilibrium** is achieved where the reactions occur at exactly the same rate in both directions. A reaction that is in equilibrium will never go to completion.

(HT) It is possible to change the position of equilibrium in a reversible reaction, as the equilibrium will shift to try to cancel out any change that is introduced to the reaction.

Increasing the concentration of the reactants in a reversible reaction means that the rate of the forward reaction will increase. This then results in a higher concentration of the products, so the rate of the reverse reaction will also increase. The rates of both reactions will eventually even out, so equilibrium is restored.

$$A + B \rightleftharpoons C + D$$

Increasing the temperature of a reversible reaction means that the reverse reaction (which is endothermic) takes in this extra heat, increasing the rate of the reverse reaction. The forward reaction (which is exothermic) gives out more heat. Eventually, the rates of both reactions even out and equilibrium is restored.

$$A + B \rightleftharpoons C + D + Heat$$

Increasing the pressure will only work in equilibrium reactions involving gases where the numbers of molecules are different. This will lead the reaction that results in the least number of molecules (i.e. the products) to release the pressure and restore equilibrium.

$$A_{(g)} + B_{(g)} \rightleftharpoons C_{(g)}$$

Ammonia

Ammonia is an alkaline gas which is lighter than air and has an unpleasant smell.

The production of ammonia and nitric acid are intermediate steps in the production of **ammonium nitrate fertiliser**, so there is great economic importance attached to getting the maximum amount of ammonia in the shortest time possible.

- A **low temperature** increases the yield of ammonia but the reaction is too slow.
- A **high pressure** increases the yield of ammonia but the reaction is too expensive.
- A **catalyst** increases the rate at which equilibrium is reached but does not affect the yield of ammonia.

Making Ammonia

Ammonia has the formula NH₃ so it consists of two elements – nitrogen and hydrogen – chemically joined together.

However, to get these gases to combine chemically, and stay combined, is very difficult because the elements combine in a reversible reaction. So, as well as nitrogen and hydrogen combining with each other, the ammonia formed also decomposes under the same conditions.

If the chemicals are in a closed system, they will reach a stage of **dynamic equilibrium** (i.e. the rate of the forward reaction is equal to the rate of the backward reaction). The word 'dynamic' is used to describe the equilibrium because there is a constant interchange between the reactants and products.

Nitrogen $+$ Hydrogen $\rightleftharpoons$ Ammonia
$N_{2(g)}$ $+$ $3H_{2(g)}$ $\rightleftharpoons$ $2NH_{3(g)}$

The Haber Process

Fritz Haber showed that ammonia could be made on a large scale, through a process which became known as the Haber process.

The raw materials are...
- nitrogen – from the fractional distillation of liquid air
- hydrogen – from natural gas and steam.

The conditions chosen are...
- temperature of 450°C – chosen in order to give a good rate of ammonia production without making it decompose too much
- pressure of 200 atmospheres – high pressure 'pushes' the equilibrium position from left to right
- iron catalyst – increases the rate at which equilibrium is reached.

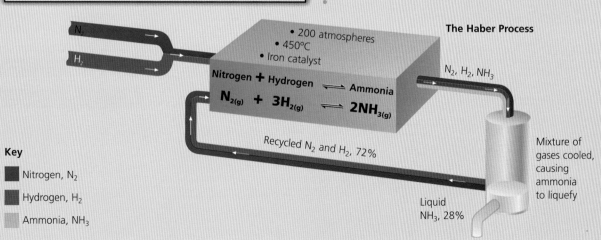

The Haber Process

- 200 atmospheres
- 450°C
- Iron catalyst

Nitrogen $+$ Hydrogen $\rightleftharpoons$ Ammonia
$N_{2(g)}$ $+$ $3H_{2(g)}$ $\rightleftharpoons$ $2NH_{3(g)}$

N_2, H_2, NH_3

Recycled N_2 and H_2, 72%

Mixture of gases cooled, causing ammonia to liquefy

Liquid NH_3, 28%

Key
- Nitrogen, N_2
- Hydrogen, H_2
- Ammonia, NH_3

How Fast? How Furious?

Fertilisers

The majority of farmers use artificial fertilisers to replace the nitrogen in the soil which has been used up by previous crops. This means that crop yields can be increased. However, organic fertilisers are now becoming more and more popular. Both artificial and organic fertilisers have advantages and disadvantages:

Artificial Fertilisers

Advantages
- Cheaper than organic fertilisers.
- Ready-made fertilisers which are specific for certain crops.

Disadvantages
- If it gets into drinking water, high nitrate content can be harmful.
- Nitrates can leak into lakes and rivers causing eutrophication (see p.22).

N.B. These disadvantages are a result of excessive use of artificial fertilisers.

Organic Fertilisers

Advantages
- Natural.
- Environmentally friendly (they do not cause pollution).

Disadvantages
- More fertiliser is needed due to low nitrogen content.
- Vary in efficiency due to the unreliability of their microorganism content.
- Need to be converted to an inorganic form by microorganisms before they can be used.
- Messy to handle.

Balancing Ionic Compounds

We can work out the formulae for ionic compounds by knowing the ions of each element in the compound. We balance the number of electrons in a compound, rather than the number of atoms.

Atoms have no overall charge because the **negatively charged electrons** balance the **positively charged protons**. When an atom loses or gains electrons, it becomes charged. This is called an **ion**.

When an atom loses electrons it forms a positively charged ion because it has lost some of the negatively charged electrons. When an atom gains electrons it forms a negatively charged ion because it has gained some of the negatively charged electrons.

However, no compound has an overall charge: the charges of the elements cancel each other out. So, we need to balance the number of electrons that have been lost and gained to make each ion. To do this, choose the lowest common multiple of the number of electrons in both ions (i.e. a number that each ion's electrons will go into).

Example

Work out the ionic equation for ammonium sulphate.

Ion for ammonium = NH_4^+ *An ammonium compound molecule that has lost 1 electron*

Ion for sulphate = SO_4^{2-} *A sulphate compound molecule that has gained 2 electrons*

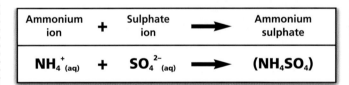

The lowest common multiple of 1 and 2 is 2. So we need to multiply the ammonium ion by 2, and the sulphate ion by 1, to make 2:

$NH_4^+ \times 2 = 2^+ = \mathbf{2NH_4^+}_{(aq)}$ *2 ammonium ions*

$SO_4^{2-} \times 1 = 2^- = \mathbf{SO_4^{2-}}_{(aq)}$ *1 sulphate ion*

This gives the ratio of ammonia ions to sulphate ions, 2:1

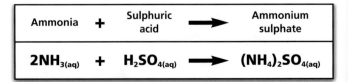

How Fast? How Furious?

Glossary

Catalyst – a substance that is used to speed up a chemical reaction without being used up in the process

Concentration – a measure of the amount of particles of a substance that are present within a specified volume of its solution; the more particles there are, the more concentrated the solution

Endothermic reaction – a chemical reaction that takes in energy from the surroundings in the form of heat

Enzymes – large protein molecules that are biological catalysts. They help reactions to take place at the low temperatures found in living organisms

Equilibrium – the state in a reversible reaction when the amount of each substance stays the same and there appears to be no change

Exothermic reaction – a chemical reaction that gives out energy to the surroundings in the form of heat

Fertiliser – a substance that is used to supplement the mineral nutrients present in soil or replace those lost through crop removal

Organic – the name given to any substance that is found in, or derived from, living things. These substances will always contain carbon

Pressure – the measure of the forces exerted due to the collision of particles of liquid or gas

Rate of reaction – the time taken for reactants to be successfully converted to products as a result of the particles colliding together

Reversible – a chemical reaction which can go either forwards or backwards: reactants react to produce products and the products can react to produce reactants

Surface area – a measure of how much surface of a solid has been exposed. Generally, the smaller the particle then the greater the overall surface area in relation to its volume

Temperature – the measure of heat

Collision theory – theory that, in order for a reaction to take place, the particles must collide with each other and those collisions must have enough energy to be successful

Dynamic equilibrium – the state in a reversible reaction when reactants are changing to products and the products are changing to reactants at the same rate. There is a constant interchange between reactants and products

Haber process – the name given to the industrial process of making ammonia from nitrogen and hydrogen

As Fast As You Can!

Speed

One way of describing the movement of an object is by measuring its **speed**, or how fast it is moving. For example…

- a cyclist travelling at a constant speed of 8 metres per second (8m/s) would travel a distance of 8 metres every second

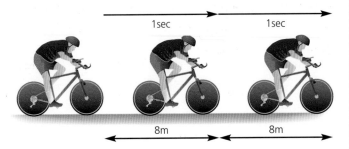

- a car travelling at a constant speed of 60 miles per hour (60mph) would travel a distance of 60 miles every hour.

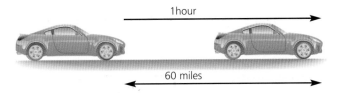

Speed is measured in **metres per second** (m/s), **kilometres per hour** (km/h) or **miles per hour** (mph).

Velocity

The **velocity** of a moving object is its speed in a stated direction, i.e. both the speed and the direction of travel. This is called a **vector quantity** (i.e. a quantity that has both size and direction).

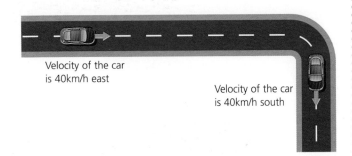

Velocity of the car is 40km/h east

Velocity of the car is 40km/h south

The car in the previous diagram may be travelling at a constant speed of 40km/h but its velocity changes because its direction of movement changes, i.e. from east to south.

The direction of velocity is usually indicated by a positive (+) or a negative (−) sign. If one car is travelling at +40mph and another is travelling at −40mph they are simply travelling in opposite directions.

We can calculate the velocity of an object using the following equation:

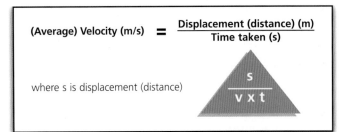

$$\text{(Average) Velocity (m/s)} = \frac{\text{Displacement (distance) (m)}}{\text{Time taken (s)}}$$

where s is displacement (distance)

Displacement is used to describe the distance covered in a certain direction. It is another vector quantity.

Example 1

A car travels 20m and then stops at a traffic light. When the lights turn green it completes its journey in 6 seconds, travelling a total of 110m from the starting point. Calculate the velocity of the second part of the journey.

> 110 − 20 = 90
> The total distance travelled in the second part of the journey

$$\text{Velocity} = \frac{\text{Displacement}}{\text{Time taken}} = \frac{110 - 20}{6} = \textbf{15m/s}$$

Example 2

An object moves a distance of 15m uniformly from rest in 5s, before returning to its starting position in 3s.

a) Calculate the velocity of the outward journey.

$$\text{Velocity} = \frac{\text{Displacement}}{\text{Time taken}} = \frac{15}{5} = \textbf{3m/s}$$

b) Calculate the velocity of the return journey.

$$\text{Velocity} = \frac{\text{Displacement}}{\text{Time taken}} = \frac{-15}{3} = \textbf{−5m/s}$$

Acceleration

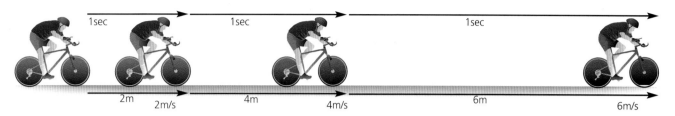

1sec   1sec   1sec

2m   4m   6m
2m/s   4m/s   6m/s

The **acceleration** of an object is the rate at which its velocity changes. In other words it is a measure of how quickly an object is speeding up or slowing down. This change can be in magnitude (size) and / or direction, so acceleration is a vector quantity.

Acceleration is measured in metres per second, per second, **m/s²**.

The cyclist in the diagram above increases his velocity by 2m/s every second. So, we can say that the acceleration of the cyclist is 2m/s² (2 metres per second, per second).

If we want to work out the acceleration of any moving object, we need to know two things:
- the change in velocity
- the time taken for the change in velocity.

We can then calculate the acceleration of the object using the following equation:

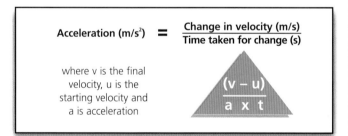

Acceleration (m/s²) = $\dfrac{\text{Change in velocity (m/s)}}{\text{Time taken for change (s)}}$

where v is the final velocity, u is the starting velocity and a is acceleration

$$\dfrac{(v - u)}{a \times t}$$

There are two important points to be aware of when measuring acceleration:

1 The cyclist in the diagram above is increasing his velocity by the **same amount every second**, however, the **distance travelled each second is increasing**.

2 **Deceleration** is simply a **negative acceleration**. In other words, it describes an object which is slowing down.

Example 1
A cyclist is travelling at a constant speed of 10m/s. He then accelerates and reaches a velocity of 24m/s after 7s. Calculate his acceleration.

$$\text{Acceleration} = \frac{\text{Change in velocity}}{\text{Time taken}}$$

$$= \frac{24 - 10}{7} = \textbf{2m/s}^2$$

Example 2
A cyclist accelerates uniformly from rest and reaches a velocity of 10m/s after 5s, before decelerating uniformly and coming to rest in a further 10s.

a) Calculate his acceleration for the first part of the journey.

$$\text{Acceleration} = \frac{\text{Change in velocity}}{\text{Time taken}}$$

$$= \frac{10 - 0}{5} = \textbf{2m/s}^2$$

b) Calculate his deceleration for the second part of the journey.

$$\text{Deceleration} = \frac{\text{Change in velocity}}{\text{Time taken}}$$

$$= \frac{0 - 10}{10} = \textbf{-1m/s}^2$$

Remember, change in velocity = final velocity – starting velocity

As Fast As You Can!

Velocity–Time Graphs

The slope of a **velocity–time graph** represents the acceleration of an object: the steeper the gradient, the greater the acceleration. The area underneath the line in a velocity–time graph represents the total distance travelled.

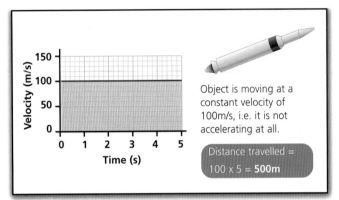

Object is moving at a constant velocity of 100m/s, i.e. it is not accelerating at all.

Distance travelled = $100 \times 5 =$ **500m**

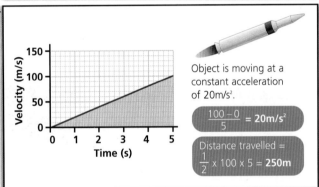

Object is moving at a constant acceleration of 20m/s².

$\frac{100-0}{5} = 20m/s^2$

Distance travelled = $\frac{1}{2} \times 100 \times 5 =$ **250m**

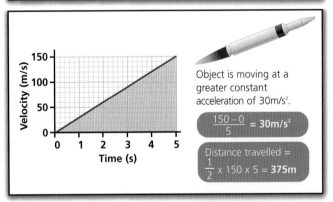

Object is moving at a greater constant acceleration of 30m/s².

$\frac{150-0}{5} = 30m/s^2$

Distance travelled = $\frac{1}{2} \times 150 \times 5 =$ **375m**

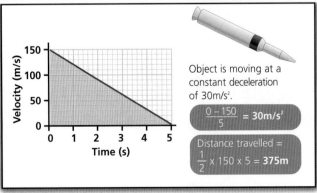

Object is moving at a constant deceleration of 30m/s².

$\frac{0-150}{5} = 30m/s^2$

Distance travelled = $\frac{1}{2} \times 150 \times 5 =$ **375m**

Forces

Forces are **pushes** or **pulls**, e.g. friction, weight and air resistance. Forces may be different in size, and act in different directions.

Force is measured in **newtons** (N).

Forces Between Two Interacting Objects

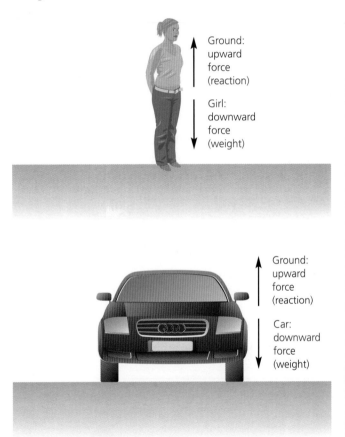

Ground: upward force (reaction)

Girl: downward force (weight)

Ground: upward force (reaction)

Car: downward force (weight)

Both the girl and the car exert a downward force (due to their weight) on the ground. The ground, in return, exerts an upward force on the girl and the car, which is **equal in size** (because nothing is moving) and **opposite in direction**.

In general, when object A pulls or pushes object B, this is called an **action force**. When object B pulls or pushes object A with a force that is equal in size and opposite in direction, this is called a **reaction force**.

So, for every action, there is an equal and opposite reaction.

How Forces Affect Movement

The movement of an object depends on all the forces acting upon it. The balance of these forces is called the **resultant force** and this force affects any subsequent motion of the object.

A moving car has forces acting on it which affect its movement:

In this diagram, the car exerts a **driving force**. The air resistance and friction are **resistive forces**. The balance of these two types of forces dictates the motion of the car. Look at the diagrams below:

1 Accelerating

When the driving force is greater than the resistive force (i.e. the resultant force is not zero), the car is accelerating. An unbalanced force acts on the car causing it to speed up, i.e. accelerate.

2 Braking

When the resistive force is greater than the driving force (i.e. the resultant force is not zero), the car is decelerating. An unbalanced force acts on the car causing it to slow down, i.e. decelerate.

3 Moving at a Constant Speed

When the driving force is equal to the resistive force (i.e. the resultant force is zero), the car is moving at a constant speed. The forces acting on the car are now balanced.

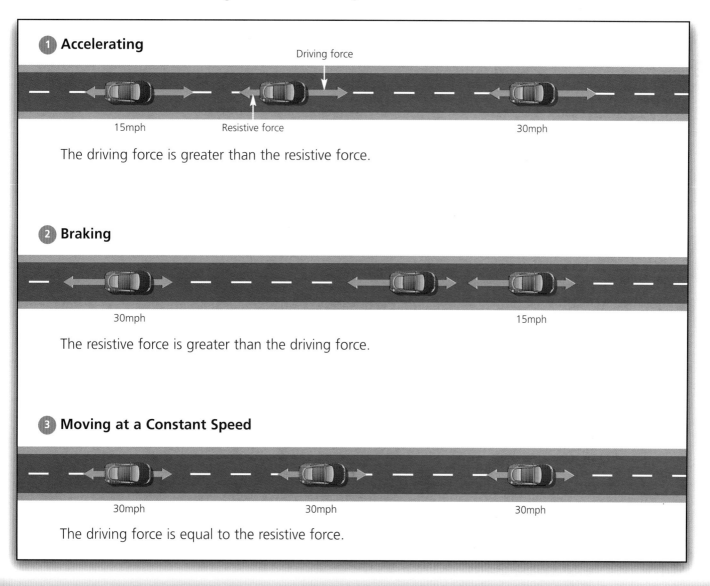

1 Accelerating

The driving force is greater than the resistive force.

2 Braking

The resistive force is greater than the driving force.

3 Moving at a Constant Speed

The driving force is equal to the resistive force.

As Fast As You Can!

Calculating Force

We can calculate an object's force using the following equation:

Resultant force (F) = Driving force – Resistive forces

Example

A car has a driving force of 3000N. It is resisted in its movement by air resistance of 150N and friction from the tyres of 850N. Calculate the resultant force for the car.

Resultant force = Driving force – Resistive forces
= 3000N – (150N + 850N)
= **2000N**

Free-body Force Diagrams

Free-body force diagrams show the forces acting on an object in equilibrium (balanced forces). Each force is shown by an arrow. The direction of the arrow indicates the direction of the force and the length of the arrow indicates the size of the force. For example...

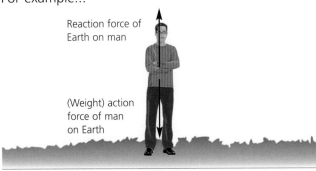

Reaction force of Earth on man

(Weight) action force of man on Earth

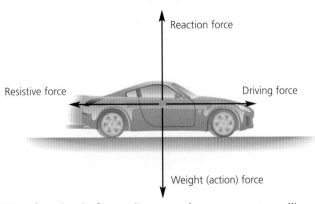

Reaction force

Resistive force

Driving force

Weight (action) force

This free-body force diagram shows a car travelling at a constant speed. The forces are all equal so the arrows are all the same length.

Force, Mass and Acceleration

If an unbalanced force acts on an object then the acceleration of the object will depend on...

- the **size** of the unbalanced force – the bigger the force, the greater the acceleration
- the **mass** of the object – the bigger the mass, the smaller the acceleration.

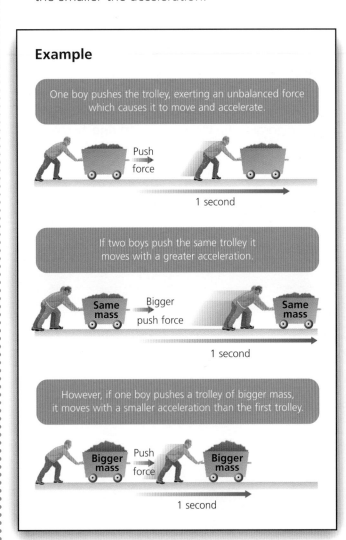

Example

One boy pushes the trolley, exerting an unbalanced force which causes it to move and accelerate.

Push force

1 second

If two boys push the same trolley it moves with a greater acceleration.

Same mass — Bigger push force — Same mass

1 second

However, if one boy pushes a trolley of bigger mass, it moves with a smaller acceleration than the first trolley.

Bigger mass — Push force — Bigger mass

1 second

The relationship between force, mass and acceleration is shown in the following formula:

$$\text{Force (N)} = \text{Mass (kg)} \times \text{Acceleration (m/s}^2)$$

$$\frac{F}{m \times a}$$

From this, we can define a newton (N) as the force needed to give a mass of one kilogram an acceleration of one metre per second squared (1m/s^2).

Example 1

A toy car of mass 800g accelerates with a force of 0.4N. Calculate its acceleration.

$$\text{Acceleration} = \frac{\text{Force}}{\text{Mass}}$$

$$= \frac{0.4\text{N}}{0.8\text{kg}}$$

Mass must be in kilograms

$$= 0.5\text{m/s}^2$$

Example 2

The trolley below, of mass 400kg, is pushed along the floor with a constant speed, by a man who exerts a push force of 150N.

Constant speed

150N

As the trolley is moving at a constant speed, the forces acting upon it must be balanced. Therefore, the 150N push force must be opposed by an equal force, i.e. 150N of friction and air resistance.

Another man joins him and the push force is increased. The trolley now accelerates at 0.5m/s^2.

Push force

Acceleration of 0.5m/s^2

Friction 150N

As the trolley is now accelerating, the push force must be greater than friction and air resistance. These forces do not cancel each other out, and an unbalanced force now acts.

a) Calculate the force needed to achieve this acceleration.

$$\text{Force} = \text{Mass} \times \text{Acceleration}$$

$$= 400\text{kg} \times 0.5\text{m/s}^2$$

$$= \textbf{200N}$$

b) Calculate the total push force exerted on the trolley.

$$\text{Total push} = \begin{array}{c}\text{Force needed to} \\ \text{equal friction and} \\ \text{air resistance}\end{array} + \begin{array}{c}\text{Force needed} \\ \text{to provide} \\ \text{acceleration}\end{array}$$

$$= 150\text{N} + 200\text{N}$$

$$= \textbf{350N}$$

What If...?

The following spreadsheet shows an example of a 'what if...?' situation. It calculates the acceleration of a car of mass 1 tonne for various driving forces.

A	B	C	D	E
Driving Forces (N)	Resistive Forces (N)	Mass of car, m (tonnes)	Resultant Forces (N)	Acceleration, a (m/s^2)
500	300	1	200	0.2
750	300	1	450	0.45
1000	300	1	700	0.7

Both the car mass and resistive forces can be altered and the acceleration re-calculated. For example, what if m (car mass) is changed?

A	B	C	D	E
Driving Forces (N)	Resistive Forces (N)	Mass of car, m (tonnes)	Resultant Forces (N)	Acceleration, a (m/s^2)
500	300	1.2	200	0.17
750	300	1.2	450	0.38
1000	300	1.2	700	0.58

Terminal Velocity

Falling objects experience two forces...
- the downward force of weight, W (↓) which always stays the same
- the upward force of air resistance, R, or drag (↑).

When a skydiver jumps out of an aeroplane, the speed of his descent can be considered in two separate parts: **before** the parachute opens and **after** the parachute opens (see diagram on p.70).

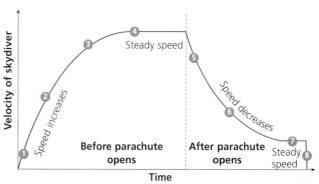

Velocity of skydiver

Speed increases

Steady speed

Speed decreases

Before parachute opens

After parachute opens

Steady speed

Time

As Fast As You Can!

Before the Parachute Opens

When the skydiver jumps, he initially accelerates due to the force of gravity (see ①). Gravity is a force of attraction that acts between bodies that have mass, e.g. the skydiver and the Earth. The weight (W) of an object is the force exerted on it by gravity. It is measured in newtons (N).

However, as the skydiver falls he experiences the frictional force of air resistance (R) in the opposite direction. But this is not as great as W so he continues to accelerate (see ②).

HT As his speed increases, so does the air resistance acting on him (see ③), until eventually R is equal to W (see ④). This means that the resultant force acting on him is now zero and his falling speed becomes constant. This speed is called the **terminal velocity**.

After the Parachute Opens

When the parachute is opened, unbalanced forces act again because the upward force of R is now greatly increased and is bigger than W (see ⑤). This causes his speed to decrease and as his speed decreases so does R (see ⑥).

Eventually R decreases until it is equal to W (see ⑦). The forces acting are once again balanced and for the second time he falls at a steady speed, slower than before though, i.e. at a **new terminal velocity**.

In the absence of air resistance, all falling bodies accelerate at the same rate. If you dropped a feather and a hammer from the same height at the same time on the Moon, both would reach the surface simultaneously.

Balanced forces and therefore constant speed

Balanced forces and therefore constant speed

Stopping Distances

The stopping distance of a vehicle depends on...

- **the thinking distance:** the distance travelled by the vehicle from the point when the driver realises he / she needs to apply the brakes to when he / she actually applies them
- **the braking distance:** the distance travelled by the vehicle from the point when the driver applies the brakes to when the vehicle actually stops.

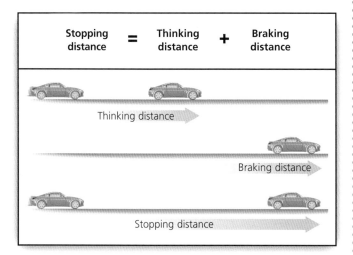

Factors Affecting Stopping Distance

The Speed of the Vehicle

The speed of the vehicle affects both the thinking distance and the braking distance. The chart below shows how the thinking distance and braking distance of a vehicle under normal driving conditions depend on the speed of the vehicle.

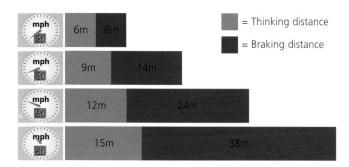

The Mass of the Vehicle

The mass of a vehicle affects the braking distance only. It has no effect on the thinking distance. If the mass of the vehicle is increased, i.e. by passengers, baggage etc., it has greater kinetic (movement) energy (see p.74), which increases the braking distance.

The Conditions of the Vehicle and the Road

The vehicle may have worn tyres, or the road conditions may be wet, icy or uneven. All these conditions will affect the friction between the tyres and the road and, therefore, the braking distance.

The Driver's Reaction Time

The driver's reaction time, i.e. the time it takes from the point the driver realises he / she needs to apply the brakes to when he / she actually applies them, affects the thinking distance only. It has no effect on the braking distance. The following would increase the reaction time of the driver:

- drinking alcohol
- taking drugs
- being tired
- being distracted by the surroundings.

Momentum

Momentum is a measure of the state of movement of an object. It is dependent on two things:

- the **mass** of the object
- the **velocity** of the object (m/s).

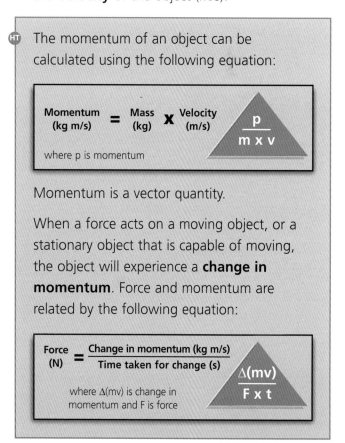

The momentum of an object can be calculated using the following equation:

$$\text{Momentum (kg m/s)} = \text{Mass (kg)} \times \text{Velocity (m/s)}$$

where p is momentum

Momentum is a vector quantity.

When a force acts on a moving object, or a stationary object that is capable of moving, the object will experience a **change in momentum**. Force and momentum are related by the following equation:

$$\text{Force (N)} = \frac{\text{Change in momentum (kg m/s)}}{\text{Time taken for change (s)}}$$

where $\Delta(mv)$ is change in momentum and F is force

As Fast As You Can!

HT Momentum (cont.)

Example 1
A railway truck with a mass of 10 tonnes is travelling with a uniform velocity of 15m/s. Calculate the truck's momentum.

Momentum = Mass x Velocity

Mass must be in kg: 1 tonne = 1000kg

= (10 x 1000)kg x 15m/s

= **150 000kg m/s**

Example 2
A car of mass 1000kg is travelling at 10m/s. 5 seconds later it is travelling at 20m/s.

a) Calculate the change in momentum.

Start momentum = 1000 x 10

= 10 000kg m/s

Finish momentum = 1000 x 20

= 20 000kg m/s

Change in momentum = 20 000 – 10 000

= **10 000kg m/s**

b) Calculate the equivalent force in newtons.

$$\text{Force} = \frac{\text{Change in momentum}}{\text{Time taken}} = \frac{10\,000}{5}$$

= **2000N**

c) Calculate the acceleration.

Force = Mass x Acceleration

$$a = \frac{F}{m} = \frac{2000}{1000} = \textbf{2m/s}^2$$

Collisions and Safety Technology

In the event of a collision, such as in a car or on a theme park ride, all of the momentum (and energy) of the impact has to be absorbed. If the momentum before impact can be reduced then the forces during impact can also be reduced (and the energy lowered). In a car, this is achieved using safety features like seatbelts, air bags and crumple zones: instead of coming to an immediate halt, there are a few seconds in which momentum is reduced. The force on the passengers is then reduced, resulting in fewer injuries.

Safety Technology

Cars have lots of safety features to try to minimise injury and reduce the number of deaths. For example...

- crumple zones within the car's structure help to absorb the momentum, meaning the force exerted on the people inside the car will be reduced, which results in fewer injuries
- power-assisted steering and anti-lock brake systems help the driver to control direction and speed which can reduce momentum
- cushioning during impact (e.g. air bags, soft seats etc.)
- seatbelts which lock when the car brakes, exerting a force to counteract the momentum of the people wearing them.

Wearing a seatbelt whilst travelling in a motor vehicle greatly reduces the chance of death in the event of an accident. In 1992, it became compulsory for all front passengers to wear seatbelts, and this led to a massive decline in the number of accident fatalities. The number was reduced again following the introduction of compulsory seatbelts for all rear passengers in 1994.

Risk Assessment

Risk is a perceived measure of the **probability of something happening**. It cannot be calculated with any degree of certainty. Risks can be **imposed** (e.g. coal mining, operating machinery) or **voluntary** (smoking, rock climbing etc.). People's perception of risk may differ widely due to their degree of familiarity with that risk. For example, a person working in a mine every day is familiar with the risk and therefore does not consider it to be as much of a risk as other people might.

As Fast As You Can!

Glossary

Acceleration – the rate at which a body increases in velocity, i.e. $\frac{\text{change in velocity}}{\text{time taken}}$

Action – a pushing or pulling force that acts on an object

Collision – an impact between two or more objects

Displacement – distance covered in a certain direction

Force – pushing or pulling action which results in an object moving, accelerating, changing direction, or remaining stationary; given by mass x acceleration; measured in newtons (N)

Gradient – a measure of how steep a line or slope is; can be positive or negative

Magnitude – a measure of size

Momentum – a measure of the state of motion of an object; given by mass x velocity (a vector quantity); measured in kg m/s

Reaction – the force that is equal in size but opposite in direction to an action

Resistance – a force that opposes motion

Resultant force – the total force acting on an object (all the forces combined)

Risk – a perceived measure of the probability of something happening

Speed – the rate at which a body moves, i.e. $\frac{\text{distance}}{\text{time taken}}$

Stopping distance – how long it takes a vehicle to stop; the sum of the thinking distance and the braking distance

Vector – a quantity that has both magnitude (size) and direction

Velocity – the speed at which an object moves in a particular direction, i.e. $\frac{\text{displacement}}{\text{time taken}}$

Velocity–time graph – represents acceleration (velocity against time taken)

Weight – the vertical force of an object; the product of mass and gravitational field strength; measured in newtons (N)

> **HT** **Terminal velocity** – the constant velocity reached by a falling body (gravitational force is equal to the frictional forces acting on it)

Roller Coasters and Relativity

Potential Energy

An object lifted above the ground gains **potential energy** (PE), often called **gravitational potential energy** (GPE). The additional height gives it the potential to do work when it falls, e.g. a diver on a diving board has gravitational potential energy.

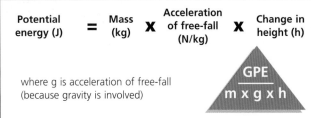

Acceleration of free-fall is also referred to as gravitational field strength (g), which (we can assume) is a constant and has a value of 10N/kg. This means that every 1kg of matter near the surface of the Earth experiences a downwards force of 10N due to gravity.

Example

A skier of mass 80kg gets on a ski lift which takes him from a height of 100m to a height of 300m above ground. By how much does his gravitational potential energy increase?

GPE = m x g x h

   = 80kg x 10N/kg x (300m – 100m)

   = 80kg x 10N/kg x 200m

   = **160 000J**

Kinetic Energy

Kinetic energy is the energy an object has because of its movement. If it is moving, it has got kinetic energy, e.g. a moving car or lorry has kinetic energy.

Example 1

A car of mass 1000kg is moving at a constant speed of 10m/s. How much kinetic energy does it have?

Kinetic energy $= \frac{1}{2}$ x Mass x Velocity^2

$= \frac{1}{2}$ x 1000kg x (10m/s)^2

$= \frac{1}{2}$ x 1000 x 100

= **50 000J**

Example 2

A lorry of mass 2050kg is moving at a constant speed of 6m/s. How much kinetic energy does it have?

Kinetic energy $= \frac{1}{2}$ x Mass x Velocity^2

$= \frac{1}{2}$ x 2050kg x (6m/s)^2

$= \frac{1}{2}$ x 2050 x 36

= **36 900J**

N.B. When a diver jumps off the diving board, or when the skier sets off down the slope, there is a transfer of energy from gravitational potential energy to kinetic energy.

Electrical Energy

The amount of **electrical energy** in an electric motor or other appliance is given by the relationship:

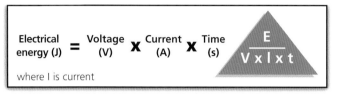

N.B. Voltage is also referred to as potential difference.

Example

Here is a simple circuit. Calculate how much energy is used if the circuit is switched on for 30 seconds.

Electrical energy = Voltage x Current x Time
            = 1.5V x 0.6A x 30s
            = **27J**

This amount of electrical energy is transferred by the bulb into other forms of energy, i.e. light and heat, during the 30 seconds.

Conservation of Energy

There are many other forms of energy: heat energy, chemical energy, nuclear energy, wave energy, sound energy etc. For example, light from the Sun can be used to produce energy through the process of photosynthesis in plants (see p.19).

The **principle of the conservation of energy** says that energy cannot be made or lost, only changed from one form into another. For example, a diver jumping off a diving board changes gravitational potential energy into kinetic energy; a hydro-electric generating plant changes gravitational potential energy into kinetic energy, then into electrical energy.

Examples of energy changes to produce electrical energy are illustrated opposite:

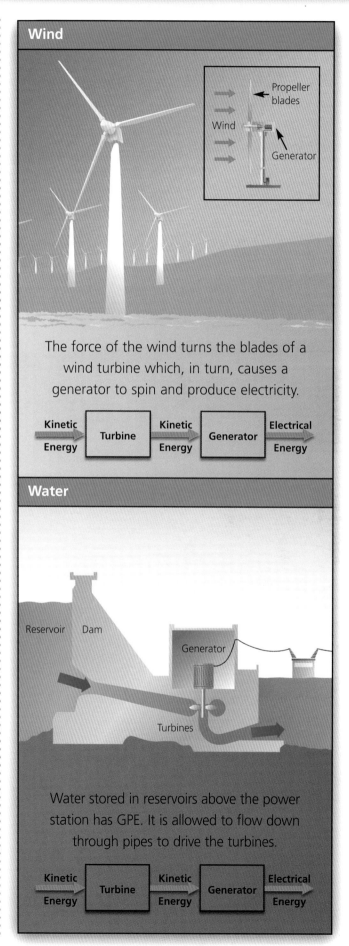

Wind

The force of the wind turns the blades of a wind turbine which, in turn, causes a generator to spin and produce electricity.

Kinetic Energy → Turbine → Kinetic Energy → Generator → Electrical Energy

Water

Water stored in reservoirs above the power station has GPE. It is allowed to flow down through pipes to drive the turbines.

Kinetic Energy → Turbine → Kinetic Energy → Generator → Electrical Energy

Roller Coasters and Relativity

Work

When a force moves an object, **work is done** on the object, resulting in the **transfer of energy** where…

> Work done (J) **=** Energy transferred (J)

Work done, force and distance moved are related by the following equation:

> $$\text{Work done (J)} = \text{Force (N)} \times \text{Distance moved in direction of force (m)}$$
>
> $$\frac{W}{F \times d}$$

Example

250N push

A man pushes a car with a steady force of 250N. The car moves a distance of 20m. How much work does the man do?

Work done = Force applied x Distance moved

   = 250N x 20m

   = 5000J (or 5kJ)

So, 5000J of **work has been done** and 5000J of **energy has been transferred**, since work done is equal to energy transferred.

Power

Power is the **rate of doing work** or the **rate of transfer of energy**. The greater the power, the more work is done every second.

Power is measured in **watts (W)** or **joules per second (J/s)**.

If two men of the same weight race up the same hill, they do the same amount of work to reach the top.

However, since one man has done the work in a **shorter time**, he has a **greater power**.

Power, work done and time taken are related by the equation:

> $$\text{Power} = \frac{\text{Work done (J)}}{\text{Time taken (s)}}$$
>
> $$\frac{W}{P \times t}$$

Example

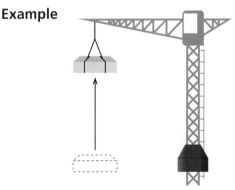

A crane lifts a load of 20 000N through a distance of 10m in 4s. Calculate the output power of the crane.

First, work out how much work the crane does against gravity, then find the power.

Work done = Force applied x Distance moved

   = 20 000N x 10m

   = 200 000J   ← The load has now gained this amount of energy

Power $= \dfrac{\text{Work done}}{\text{Time taken}}$

   $= \dfrac{200\,000\text{J}}{4\text{s}}$

   = 50 000W (or J/s)

Or **P = 50kW**, since 1kW = 1000W

Circular Motion

If you swing a rubber ball attached to a piece of string in a horizontal circle at a constant speed, the direction of the ball is always changing. This means that the velocity of the ball (remember velocity is a vector) is also changing (in direction only), so the ball must be undergoing constant acceleration.

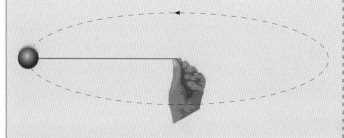

Centripetal Force

Newton's Law connects an acceleration, a, with a force, F:

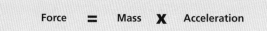

Force	=	Mass	X	Acceleration

The acceleration is brought about by a resultant force acting on the object. The resultant force that acts on the ball to keep it moving in a circular path is an **inward centripetal force**, in this case, the tension in the string.

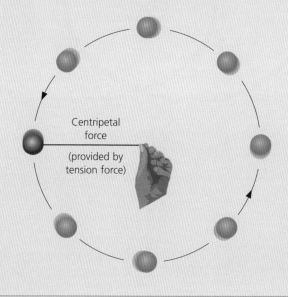

Centripetal force
(provided by tension force)

The same principle can be applied to the Moon and satellites in orbit around the Earth, or the Earth moving in orbit around the Sun.

In these cases, objects are kept in orbit by the **inward gravitational force** of the Earth (the Moon and satellites in orbit), or of the Sun (the Earth in orbit).

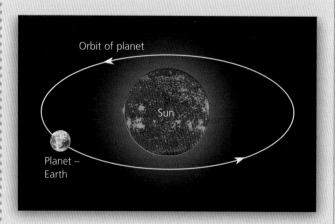

Orbit of planet

Sun

Planet – Earth

The inward force involved is greater if…
- the mass of the object increases
- the speed (or velocity) of the object increases
- the radius of the circle decreases.

If the force suddenly stops (e.g. the string snaps) the object moves off in a straight line at a tangent to the circle. It does not move outwards.

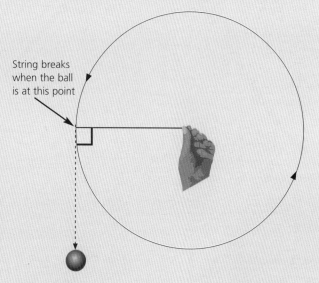

String breaks when the ball is at this point

Centripetal forces act in all cases of circular motion, for example, a car driving around a corner, the loop of a roller coaster ride etc.

Roller Coasters and Relativity

Roller Coasters

We can use the terms speed, acceleration, force and energy to describe how a roller coaster ride works.

The initial lift in a roller coaster serves to build up gravitational potential energy (GPE). After reaching its highest point, the roller coaster starts down the first hill where gravity takes over and the gravitational potential energy begins to change into kinetic energy (KE).

Gravity, together with the mass of the cars and the passengers, applies a constant downward force which makes the cars accelerate down the hill. The roller coaster track simply serves to channel this force.

The initial height gained by the roller coaster dictates the size and shape of the remainder of the ride. The more gravitational potential energy that is built up in the initial lift, the more kinetic energy is produced for the rest of the ride, and the faster the speed of the ride.

Converting Energy

A roller coaster's energy is constantly changing between potential and kinetic energy, and the straight and curved sections (short sections of circular motion at the top of a stage or in a dip) only serve to heighten the acceleration, speed and forces experienced.

1. On most roller coasters the cars start high up with a lot of gravitational potential energy (or they are lifted mechanically, building up gravitational energy).
2. As the cars drop, the gravitational potential energy is gradually being transferred into kinetic energy.
3. The car accelerates to reach its highest speed (maximum kinetic energy) at the bottom of the slope.
4. As the car climbs the slope on the other side, kinetic energy is converted back into gravitational potential energy.

The height of any other hills or loops in the ride will always be less than the height of the initial one.

Maximum GPE – lowest speed

Maximum centripetal force – GPE increases

Initial lift to maximise GPE

Cars speed up – GPE turns into KE

Cars speed up – GPE turns into KE

Maximum KE – greatest speed

Cars slow down – KE turns into GPE

Roller Coasters and Relativity

Relativity

Albert Einstein devised…

- the Special Theory of Relativity (which led to the famous equation $E = mc^2$, i.e. energy = mass x speed of light x speed of light)
- the General Theory of Relativity.

Relativity Theory

Relativity theory refers to the idea that time and space are relative concepts (i.e. they are dependent on something else).

Special Relativity Theory

Special relativity theory, proposed by Einstein in 1905, challenged the accepted ideas at that time and led to predictions that differed from those of Isaac Newton. The theory is based on the ideas that…

- all movement is relative (e.g. someone may be sitting still, but 'still' relative to what?)
- light has a constant speed (i.e. 300 000 000km per second) in a particular direction
- the speed of light from a constantly moving source is always the same, regardless of how fast or slow the source or the observer is moving.

General Relativity Theory

General relativity theory expanded on special relativity theory by looking at the effects of gravity and accelerated motion. It is based on the ideas that…

- gravitational force is equal to inertial force (i.e. the force of an object which is either still, or which is moving at a constant speed in a particular direction)
- a gravitational field can bend light
- a strong gravitational field can slow things down.

Einstein's General Theory of Relativity was proven by three careful observations:

1 The slow movement of Mercury's axis as it orbits the Sun. This tiny effect was confirmed by very precise measurements.

2 Light can be bent. Precise observations indicated that he was right, both about the effect and size.

3 Light coming from a strong gravitational area can be shifted in wavelength. Detailed observations showed that this so-called 'red shift' was correct and of the correct size.

HT Einstein's theory of relativity was accepted as a result of successful tests.

One of Einstein's predictions in his theory of relativity stated that time is affected by gravity and, therefore, clocks in strong gravity tick slower than clocks in weaker gravity. An experiment in which **atomic clocks** (very accurate) were placed at different distances from the surface of the Earth (therefore at different gravitational strengths), proved this theory.

Another of Einstein's predictions on time slowing down was experimentally proven by looking at high energy **cosmic rays** that enter the Earth's atmosphere from space. As they are moving close to the speed of light, the count rate (average number of radioactive emissions) increased. This increase in count rate could only be explained using Einstein's theory.

Like other scientists, Einstein initially explained his ideas using only **thought experiments** (i.e. imagination). His theories did not emerge as the result of experimental data. It was only much later that experimental proof was provided through careful experimental observations.

Some scientists are often reluctant to accept new theories, such as Einstein's theory of relativity, because they overturn long-established explanations. Scientists may have carried out a lot of work and research based on other explanations, which they do not want to simply dismiss.

Theories such as Einstein's can also be difficult to prove, meaning that some scientists are more likely to continue basing their work on the long-established, accepted explanation.

Roller Coasters and Relativity

Glossary

Acceleration – the rate at which a body increases in velocity, i.e. $\frac{\text{change in velocity}}{\text{time taken}}$

Centripetal force – the constant inward force of an object which causes it to move in a circular path

Conservation of energy – a law that states that energy cannot be made or lost: it can only be changed from one form into another

Constant speed – the speed of an object that is neither accelerating nor decelerating

Current – the rate of flow of an electrical charge; measured in amperes (A)

Distance – the space between two points

Electrical energy – energy of electric charges or current; the product of the voltage (volts), current (amps) and time (s); measured in joules (J)

Energy transfer – a measure of the amount of electrical energy transferred

Force – a push or pull acting on an object

Gravitational potential energy (GPE) – one form of potential energy: the product of the weight of an object and its change in height; measured in joules (J)

Kinetic energy (KE) – the energy possessed by a moving object; measured in joules (J)

Mass – the quantity of matter in an object

Potential energy (PE) – the energy stored in an object as a consequence of its position, shape or state (includes gravitational, electrical, nuclear and chemical); measured in joules (J)

Potential difference (p.d.) – same as voltage: difference in electrical charge between two charged points; expressed in volts (V)

Power – the rate of doing work or the rate of transfer of energy; measured in joules per second (J/s) or watts (W)

Theory of relativity – the theory that space and time are relative. The Special and General Theories were proposed by Albert Einstein and extended the work of Isaac Newton

Resultant force – the total force acting on an object (all the forces combined)

Speed – the rate at which a body moves, i.e. $\frac{\text{distance}}{\text{time taken}}$

Vector quantity – a quantity in which both the size (magnitude) and direction must be given

Velocity – the speed at which an object moves in a particular direction

Voltage – same as potential difference: the difference in electrical charge between two charged points; expressed in volts (V)

Weight – the vertical force of an object; the product of mass and gravitational field strength; measured in newtons (N)

Work – the energy transfer that occurs when a force causes an object to move a certain distance

Work done – the product of the force applied to a body and the distance moved in the direction of the force; measured in joules (J)

The Atom

Atoms are basic particles from which all matter is made up. All chemical elements are made of atoms.

Atoms have a small nucleus consisting of **protons** (positively charged), and **neutrons** (neutral). The nucleus is surrounded by electrons (negatively charged) (see p.41).

The **mass number (or nucleon number)** of an element is the total number of protons and neutrons in the nucleus of an atom.

The **atomic number (or proton number)** of an element is the number of protons (or electrons) in the nucleus of an atom.

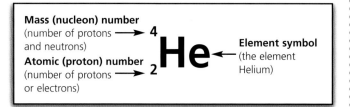

Mass (nucleon) number (number of protons and neutrons) → 4
Atomic (proton) number (number of protons or electrons) → 2
$^{4}_{2}\text{He}$
Element symbol (the element Helium)

Isotopes

All atoms of a particular element have the same number of protons. The number of protons defines the element. However, some atoms of the same element can have different numbers of neutrons – these are called **isotopes**. Oxygen has three isotopes:

① $^{16}_{8}\text{O}$ 8 neutrons   ② $^{17}_{8}\text{O}$ 9 neutrons   ③ $^{18}_{8}\text{O}$ 10 neutrons

> **HT** Although the atomic (proton) number is the same in all isotopes of an element, the mass (nucleon) number will vary, and tells us how many neutrons there are in each isotope of the element.

Radiation

Some substances contain isotopes with **unstable nuclei**. An atom is unstable when its nucleus contains too many or too few neutrons.

Unstable nuclei split up or disintegrate, emitting

radiation. The atoms of such isotopes disintegrate randomly and are said to be **radioactive**.

There are three main types of radioactive radiation:
- **Alpha (α)** – an alpha particle is a helium nucleus (a particle made up of two protons and two neutrons).
- **Beta (β)** – a beta particle is a high-energy electron.
- **Gamma (γ)** – a gamma ray is high-frequency electromagnetic radiation.

A radioactive isotope will emit one of the three types of radiation from its nucleus.

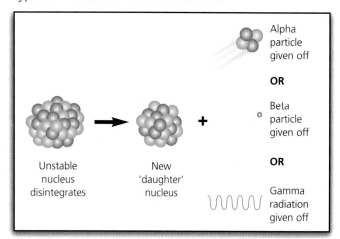

Unstable nucleus disintegrates → New 'daughter' nucleus +

Alpha particle given off

OR

Beta particle given off

OR

Gamma radiation given off

The **activity** of a radioactive isotope is the average number of disintegrations that occur every second. It is measured in **becquerels** and decreases over a period of time.

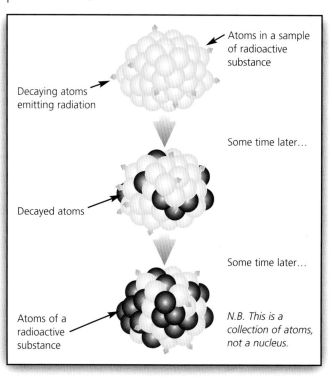

Atoms in a sample of radioactive substance

Decaying atoms emitting radiation

Some time later...

Decayed atoms

Some time later...

Atoms of a radioactive substance

N.B. This is a collection of atoms, not a nucleus.

Putting Radiation to Use

Half-life

The **half-life** of a radioactive isotope is a measurement of the rate of radioactive decay, i.e. the time it takes for half the nuclei to decay.

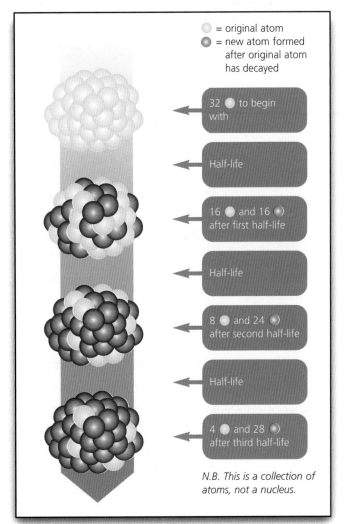

○ = original atom

◉ = new atom formed after original atom has decayed

32 ◉ to begin with

Half-life

16 ◉ and 16 ◉ after first half-life

Half-life

8 ◉ and 24 ◉ after second half-life

Half-life

4 ◉ and 28 ◉ after third half-life

N.B. This is a collection of atoms, not a nucleus.

If a radioactive isotope has a very long half-life, then it remains active for a very long time.

The graph below shows the count rate against time for the radioactive material iodine-128. The count rate is the average number of radioactive emissions.

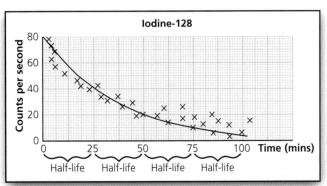

As time goes on there are fewer and fewer unstable atoms left to decay. After 25 minutes the count rate has fallen to half its original value. Therefore, iodine-128 has a half-life of 25 minutes.

The table below shows the half-lives of some other radioactive elements.

Material	Half-life
Radon-222	4 days
Strontium-90	28 years
Radium-226	1600 years
Carbon-14	5730 years
Plutonium-239	24 400 years
Uranium-235	700 000 000 years

Using Half-life

Knowledge about the half-lives of radioactive elements can be used to date certain materials by measuring the amount of radiation they emit.

Materials which can be dated include…
- very old samples of wood
- remains of prehistoric bones
- certain types of rock.

This is because certain materials contain radioactive isotopes which decay to produce **stable isotopes**. If we know the **proportion** of each of these isotopes and the half-life of the radioactive isotope, then it is possible to date the material. For example…
- igneous rocks may contain uranium isotopes which decay via a series of relatively short-lived isotopes to produce stable isotopes of lead. This takes a long time because uranium has a very long half-life
- wood and bones contain the carbon-14 isotope which decays when the organism dies.

Radiation Calculations

Example 1

A very small sample of dead wood has an activity of 1000 becquerels over a period of time. The same mass of 'live' wood has an activity of 4000 becquerels over an identical period of time. If the half-life of carbon-14 is 5730 years, calculate the age of the wood.

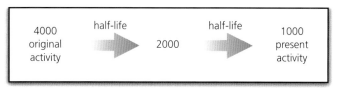

Therefore the carbon-14 has taken 2 x half-lives to decay to its present activity.

So, the age of the wood = 2 x 5730 years

$$= \textbf{11 460 years.}$$

Example 2

A sample of igneous rock is found to contain three times as much lead as uranium. If the half-life of uranium is 700 000 000 years, calculate the age of the rock.

The fraction of lead present is $\frac{3}{4}$ while that of uranium is $\frac{1}{4}$ (there is three times as much lead as uranium).

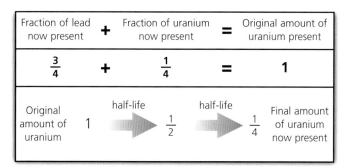

So, the age of the rock = 2 x half-life
= 2 x 700 000 000
= **1 400 000 000 years**
(1 400 million years)

Radiation and Ionisation

A radioactive substance is capable of emitting one of the three types of radiation: **alpha, beta** or **gamma**. When this radiation collides with neutral atoms or molecules in a substance, the atoms or molecules may become charged due to electrons being 'knocked out' of their structure during the collision. This alters their structure, leaving them as **ions** (atoms with an electrical charge) or **charged particles**.

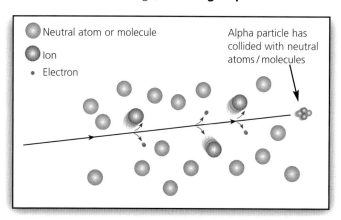

HT Alpha particles, beta particles and gamma rays are therefore known as **ionising radiations** (they are randomly emitted from the unstable nuclei of radioactive isotopes).

The relative ionising power of each type of radiation is different, as is its power to penetrate different materials, and its range in air.

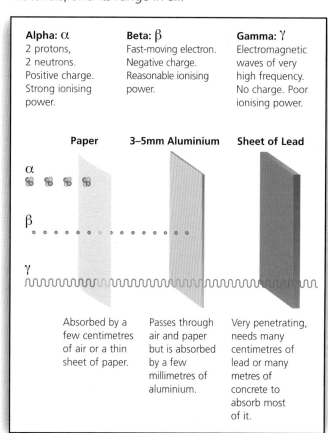

Putting Radiation to Use

Effect of Ionising Radiation on Living Organisms

Ionising radiation can damage cells and tissues, causing cancer, including leukaemia (cancer of the blood), or mutations (changes) in the cells, and can result in the birth of deformed babies in future generations. This is why precautions must always be taken when dealing with any type of radiation.

With all types of radiation, the greater the dose received, the greater the risk of damage. However, the damaging effect depends on whether the radiation source is outside or inside the body.

If the source is outside the body...

- alpha (α) radiation is stopped by the skin and cannot penetrate into the body
- beta (β) and gamma (γ) radiation and X-rays can penetrate into the body to reach the cells of organs where they are absorbed.

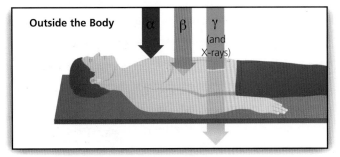

If the source is inside the body...

- alpha (α) radiation causes most damage as it is strongly absorbed by cells, causing the most ionisation
- beta (β) and gamma (γ) radiation and X-rays cause less damage as they are less likely to be absorbed by cells.

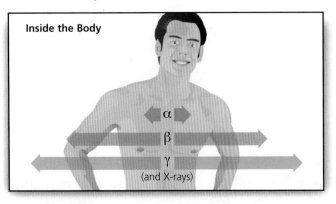

Ionising radiation can be used beneficially, for example, to treat tumours and cancers. This is done by one of the following methods:

- implanting a radioactive material in the area to be treated
- dosing the patient with a radioactive isotope
- exposing the patient to precisely focused beams of radiation from a machine such as an X-ray machine or gamma-camera.

Radiotherapy slows down the spread of cancerous cells so it is used to treat cancer.

Gamma Rays and X-rays

Gamma rays and X-rays are forms of electromagnetic radiation. Gamma rays are emitted by highly excited atomic nuclei. X-rays can be produced using a medical X-ray tube and are emitted when fast-moving electrons hit a metal target. Low energy gamma rays and X-rays can pass through flesh but not bone, which is why bones show up on an X-ray photograph. Gamma rays and X-rays have weak ionising power and both can damage living cells.

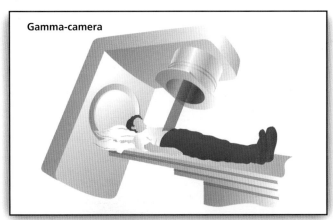

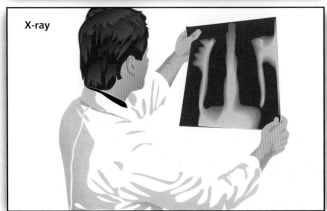

Putting Radiation to Use

Uses of Radiation

Controlling the Thickness of Sheet Materials

When radiation passes through a material, some of it is absorbed. The greater the thickness of the material, the greater the absorption of radiation. This can be used to control the thickness of different manufactured materials, e.g. paper production at a paper mill. If the paper is too thick then less radiation passes through to the detector and a signal is sent to the rollers which move closer together.

A beta emitter is used since the paper would absorb all alpha particles and would have no effect at all on gamma rays, regardless of its thickness.

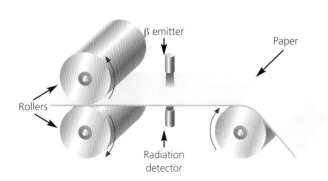

Smoke Detectors

Most smoke alarms contain americium-241 which is an alpha emitter. Emitted alpha particles cause ionisation of the air particles and the ions formed are attracted to the oppositely charged electrodes. This results in a current flowing through the circuit.

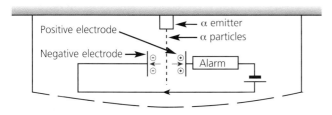

When smoke enters the space between the two electrodes, less ionisation takes place as the alpha particles are absorbed by the smoke particles. A smaller current than normal flows causing the alarm to sound.

Sterilisation of Medical Instruments

Gamma rays can be used to sterilise medical instruments because germs and bacteria are destroyed by them. An advantage of this method is that no heat is required, therefore damage to the instruments is minimised.

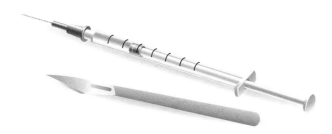

Preserving Food

Subjecting food to low doses of radiation kills microorganisms within the food and prolongs its shelf life.

Radioactive (Carbon) Dating

Radioactive carbon dating looks at the amount of radioactive carbon-14 that decays to form nitrogen. It is based on a constant cosmic background (background radiation from space) and has been shown to give consistent results for materials up to 40 000 years old.

The accuracy depends on the assumption that the cosmic background has remained the same throughout this period of time, so carbon dating does carry uncertainties.

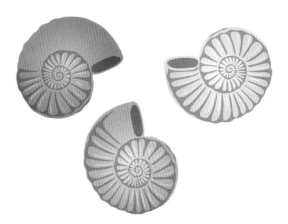

Such uses demonstrate how scientific ideas and knowledge about the risks and benefits associated with radioactive sources, have developed over time.

Putting Radiation to Use

Background Radiation

Background radiation is radiation that occurs naturally all around us. It only provides a very small dose so there is no danger to our health. The pie chart below shows the sources of background radiation.

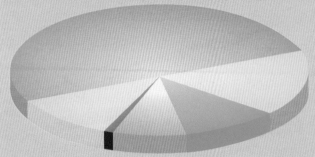

Key:

■ **Radon gas (50%)**
A colourless, odourless gas produced during the radioactive decay of uranium which is found naturally in granite rock. Released at the surface of the ground, it poses a threat if it builds up in a home, e.g. it can result in lung cancer. The amount of radon varies. Areas with higher concentrations tend to be built on granite, e.g. Devon and Cornwall.

■ **Medical (12%)**
Mainly X-rays.

■ **Nuclear industry (less than 1%)**

■ **Cosmic rays (10%)**
From outer space and the Sun.

■ **Gamma (γ) rays (15%)**
From rock, soil and building products.

■ **From food (12%)**

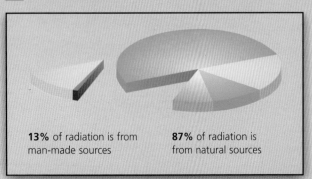

13% of radiation is from man-made sources   **87%** of radiation is from natural sources

Protecting the Earth

The Earth is surrounded by various layers of gas that shield and protect the Earth from radiation coming from space by reflecting the radiation back into space.

Exosphere – 400km+ from the Earth's surface
Thermosphere – 300km from the Earth's surface
Mesosphere – 50km from the Earth's surface
Stratosphere – 40km from the Earth's surface
Troposphere – 10km from the Earth's surface

In addition, the Earth's own magnetic field (the geomagnetic field) also protects us from the high-speed solar wind that comes from the Sun. This magnetic field provides an invisible barrier to the charged particles that stream towards us and which are reflected by the field.

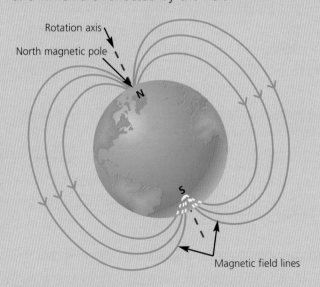

Rotation axis
North magnetic pole
Magnetic field lines

Without the atmospheric and magnetic fields, life on Earth would not be possible.

Putting Radiation to Use

Glossary

Activity – the average number of disintegrations that occur every second in the nuclei of radioactive substances; measured in Becquerels

Alpha particles – consist of two protons and two neutrons (a helium nucleus); emitted from the nuclei of radioactive substances during alpha decay

Atom – the smallest part of an element that displays the chemical property of the element; consists of a small central nucleus (containing protons and neutrons), surrounded by electrons

Atomic mass – the mass of atoms compared to that of the mass of the carbon-12 atom

Atomic proton number – the number of protons in the nucleus of an atom

Becquerel – the unit of radioactivity; one nuclear disintegration per second

Beta particles – fast-moving electrons; emitted from the nuclei of radioactive substances during beta decay

Daughter nucleus – a nucleus produced by radioactive decay of another nucleus (the parent)

Dose – a measure of the extent to which matter has been exposed to ionising radiation

Electron – a negatively charged subatomic particle with a very tiny mass

Gamma ray – electromagnetic radiation of a very high frequency emitted by excited nuclei

Half-life – the time taken for half of the undecayed nuclei in radioactive material to decay

Ionisation – the charging of neutral atoms or molecules when radiation collides with their electrons

Ionising radiation – a stream of high-energy particles / rays: alpha, beta, gamma; can damage human cells and tissues

Isotopes – atoms of the same element that have the same number of protons but a different number of neutrons

Mutations – changes in the structure of living cells

Neutron – a neutrally charged subatomic particle with the same mass as a proton

Nucleus – the centre of an atom containing protons and neutrons

Mass (nucleon) number – the total number of protons and neutrons (nucleons) in the nucleus of an atom

Proton – a positively charged subatomic particle with the same mass as a neutron

Radiation – electromagnetic particles / rays (e.g. alpha, beta, gamma) emitted by a radioactive substance

Radioactive – materials containing unstable nuclei that spontaneously decay

Radioactive dating – a method of estimating the ages of ancient objects based on carbon-14 (for wood / bones) and uranium (for rocks)

Radioactivity – the emission of high-energy particles / rays from the spontaneous decay of unstable nuclei

Radiotherapy – the use of ionising radiation in the treatment of cancer

Radon gas – a colourless radioactive gas that occurs naturally

Sterilisation – destroying germs and bacteria by exposure to gamma rays

Unstable nuclei – found in atoms that disintegrate; they emit radiation

X-rays – a form of electromagnetic radiation used in industry and medicine

---

(HT) **Background radiation** – radiation from natural sources in the environment

Magnetic field – a field of force that exists around a magnetic body

Power of the Atom

Energy Trapped Inside the Atom

Large, **heavy** atoms, like atoms of uranium, can become more stable by losing an alpha or beta particle, a process which occurs naturally. Stability can be gained more quickly by bombarding the nucleus of the atom of uranium with neutrons in a process called **nuclear fission**. The tiny amount of mass lost in the fission process is translated into an enormous energy gain according to Einstein's famous equation connecting energy (E) with mass (m) through the speed of light (c):

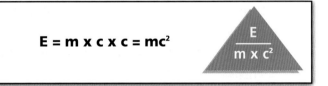

$$E = m \times c \times c = mc^2$$

$$\frac{E}{m \times c^2}$$

Einstein's predicted energy release was verified in 1943 when the first atomic bomb test was carried out.

Nuclear Fission

Nuclear fission is the process of **splitting atomic nuclei**. It is used in nuclear reactors to produce energy to make electricity (see p.89). The two substances commonly used are uranium-235 (U-235) and plutonium-239 (P-239). Unlike radioactive decay, which is a random process, nuclear fission is caused by the bombardment of the atom's nucleus with a source of neutrons.

The products of the collision are two smaller nuclei and two or three other neutrons along with the release of an enormous amount of energy. If 235g of U-235 were fissioned, the energy produced would be the same as burning 800 000kg of coal!

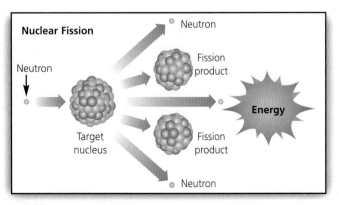

The products of nuclear fission are radioactive, and remain radioactive for a long time, which means they must be stored or disposed of very carefully.

Some radioactive waste can be reprocessed but often it has to be disposed of. Low-level waste is sealed and buried in landfill sites but higher-level waste is mixed with sugar, bonded with glass, poured into steel cylinders and kept underground.

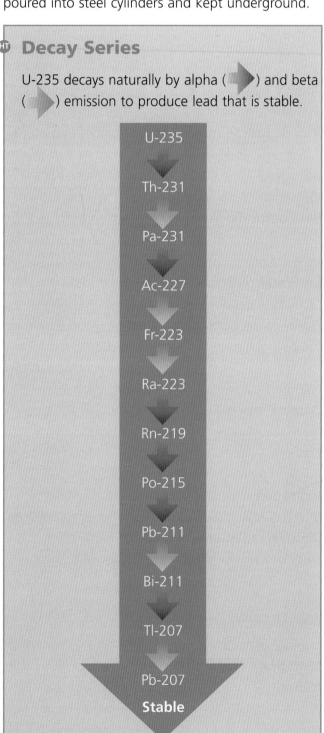

Chain Reactions

The Chain Reaction of U-235

A single neutron colliding with a U-235 nucleus produces two further neutrons. These neutrons can go on to interact with further U-235 nuclei, producing four neutrons, then eight, then 16, then 32 and so on. Each fission reaction produces an enormous amount of energy in a process called a **chain reaction**.

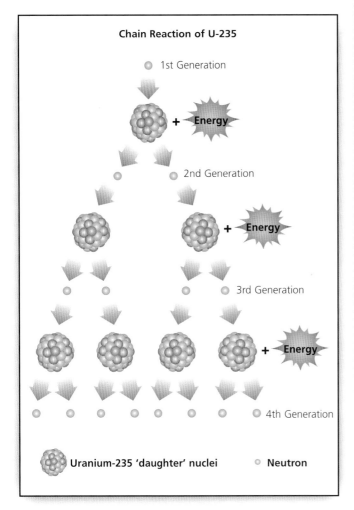

Chain Reaction of U-235

Atomic Bombs and Nuclear Reactors

Manipulating the chain reaction allows it to be used in two different ways:

1 Uncontrolled Chain Reaction
- Neutrons bombard pure uranium nuclei.
- An enormous amount of energy is released.
- An enormous amount of radiation is released.

This forms an **atomic bomb**.

2 Controlled Chain Reaction
- Neutrons bombard a mixture of U-235 and U-238 nuclei.
- The heat produced is used to make steam to generate electricity.

This forms a **nuclear reactor**.

Nuclear Reactors

The diagram below shows a **pressurised water reactor (PWR)**. The reactor is inside a steel pressure vessel and is surrounded by thick concrete to absorb radiation. Heat (thermal energy) from the PWR is carried away by water that is boiled to produce steam. The steam drives the turbines that generate electricity (electrical energy). The steam cools to produce water which is then returned to the reactor to be re-heated.

The reactor cannot explode like an atomic bomb because the U-235 nuclei are too far apart for an uncontrolled chain reaction to occur.

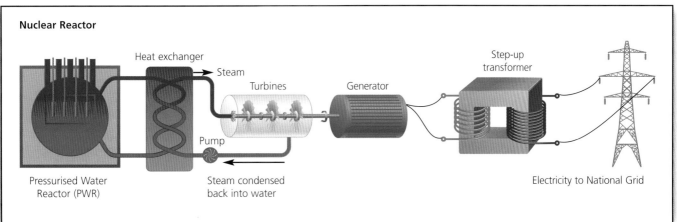

Nuclear Reactor

Power of the Atom

Environmental and Social Impacts

The use of **nuclear power** has advantages and disadvantages, and the setting up of a nuclear power station in any part of the UK will have a huge environmental and social impact.

Advantages of a Nuclear Power Station

- No greenhouse gas emissions (e.g. carbon dioxide).
- No air pollutants like carbon monoxide, sulphur dioxide etc.
- Quantity of waste is small.
- Low fuel costs.
- Local economy could benefit from the many jobs created.

Disadvantages of a Nuclear Power Station

- Risk of a major accident, e.g. Six Mile Island, Chernobyl.
- Nuclear waste is dangerous and long-lived leading to transport and storage problems.
- High construction and maintenance costs.
- Security concerns.
- Large-scale designs – large areas of land used.
- A power station spoils the look of the countryside.
- Wildlife habitats would be destroyed.
- An increase in traffic means an increase in noise and air pollution.

ⓗ Nuclear Fusion

Nuclear fusion involves the joining together of two or more atomic nuclei to form a larger atomic nucleus. It takes a huge amount of heat and energy to force the nuclei to fuse. This means that fusion is not a practical way to generate power. However, the energy produced by fusion is much greater than that produced by fission and, if we could somehow harness the energy from fusion, we would have unlimited amounts of energy and our energy problems would be solved.

The energy produced by the Sun, and similar stars, comes from the fusion of two 'heavy' isotopes of hydrogen called **deuterium** and **tritium**.

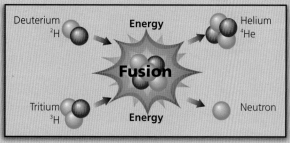

To push and join the two nuclei together is difficult and requires very high temperatures, high pressures and high densities, similar to those found in the Sun. In the core of the Sun (and similar stars), hydrogen is converted to helium by fusion. This provides the energy to keep the Sun, and the other stars, burning.

Cold Fusion

A large amount of work is currently being done on the theory of the process of **cold fusion**. Cold fusion would occur at much lower temperatures than ordinary fusion, in order to overcome the repulsive forces between nuclei (different nuclei to those involved in ordinary fusion). However, scientific theories such as this are often not accepted until they have been validated by the scientific community (i.e. proven by a number of scientists).

Static Electricity

Materials that allow electricity to flow through them easily are called **electrical conductors**. Metals are good electrical conductors. Plastics and many other materials, on the other hand, do not allow electricity to flow through them; they are called **insulators**.

However, it is possible for an insulator to become electrically charged if there is friction between it and another insulator. When this happens, electrons are transferred from one material to the other. The insulator is then charged with **static electricity**. It is called 'static' because the electricity stays on the material and does not move.

You can generate static electricity by rubbing a balloon against your jumper. The electrically charged balloon will then attract very small objects.

Electric charge (static) builds up when electrons (which have a negative charge) are rubbed off one material onto another. The material **receiving electrons** becomes **negatively charged** and the one **giving up electrons** becomes **positively charged**.

For example, if you rub a Perspex rod with a cloth, it loses electrons to become positively charged. The cloth gains electrons to become negatively charged.

If you rub an ebonite rod with a fur, it gains electrons to become negatively charged. The fur loses electrons to become positively charged.

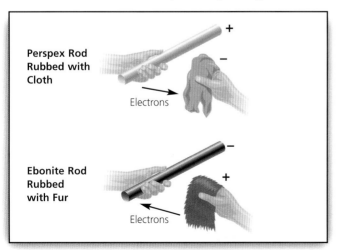

Perspex Rod Rubbed with Cloth — Electrons

Ebonite Rod Rubbed with Fur — Electrons

Repulsion and Attraction

When two charged materials are brought together, they exert a force on each other so they are **attracted** or **repelled**. Two materials with the **same type of charge repel each other**; two materials **with different types of charge attract each other**.

If you move an ebonite rod near to a suspended Perspex rod, the suspended Perspex rod will be attracted.

If you move a Perspex rod near to a suspended Perspex rod, the suspended Perspex rod will be repelled.

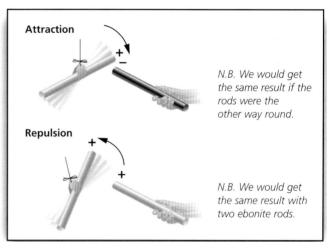

Attraction

N.B. We would get the same result if the rods were the other way round.

Repulsion

N.B. We would get the same result with two ebonite rods.

Common Electrostatic Phenomena

The following all involve the movement of electrons:

1. Lightning: clouds become charged up by rising hot air until discharge occurs, i.e. a bolt of lightning.
2. Charges on synthetic fabrics: static sparks when synthetic clothing is removed from the body.
3. Shocks from car doors: a car can become charged up due to friction between itself and air when it moves.

Power of the Atom

Using Static in Everyday Life

The Laser Printer

An image of the page to be copied is projected onto an electrically charged plate (usually positively charged).

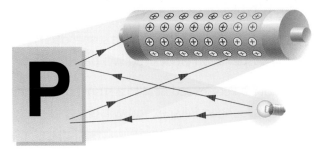

Light causes charge to leak away leaving an electrostatic impression of the page.

This charged impression on the plate attracts tiny specks of black powder, which is then transferred from the plate to the paper. Heat is used to fix the final image on the paper.

Fingerprinting

The semiconductor fingerprint sensor measures the electrostatic charge between the sensor surface and the skin. Fingerprints are patterns of ridges and valleys in the skin. Ridges give high electrostatic charges and valleys give small electrostatic charges and these are copied directly onto the sensor.

The technique, although new, is sensitive to changes in the environment such as static electricity and temperature.

Discharging Unsafe Static

Filling Aircraft Fuel Tanks

During refuelling, the fuel gains electrons from the fuel pipe, making the pipe positively charged and the fuel negatively charged. The resulting voltage between the two can cause a spark (discharge), which could cause a huge explosion. To prevent this, either of the following can be done:

- the fuel tank can be earthed with a copper conductor
- the tanker and the plane can be linked with a copper conductor.

Earthing

Earthing allows a constant safe discharge to occur, to equalise the electron imbalance between the two objects. When earthing occurs, electrons flow from one body to the other to remove the imbalance.

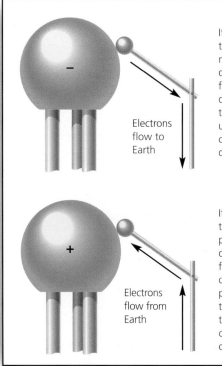

If a conductor touches a negatively charged dome, electrons flow from the dome to Earth, via the conductor, until the dome is completely discharged.

Electrons flow to Earth

If a conductor touches a positively charged dome, electrons flow from Earth to cancel out the positive charge on the dome, until the dome is completely discharged.

Electrons flow from Earth

Power of the Atom

Glossary

Attraction – the drawing together of two materials with different charges

Chain reaction – a self-sustaining series of reactions, like nuclear fission, in which the neutrons released in one fission trigger the fission of other nuclei

Cold fusion – the joining together of atomic nuclei at low temperatures to produce energy

Daughter nucleus – a nucleus that is produced by the radioactive decay of another nucleus (i.e. a larger, parent nucleus)

Earthing – allows electrons to flow from one object to another to encourage discharge

Electrical conductor – a material that allows electricity (and heat) to flow through it easily

Electrical energy – a form of energy given by the product of the electric charge and the potential difference (voltage)

Electrostatic – the stationary electric field that surrounds a charged object; caused by friction

Nuclear fission – the splitting of atomic nuclei that produces a large amount of energy

Insulation – when electricity (or heat) cannot flow easily

Insulator – a material that does not allow electricity (or heat) to flow through it easily

Nucleus – the core of an atom; contains protons and neutrons

Neutron – a neutrally charged subatomic particle found in the nucleus of an atom

Nuclear reactor – a device in which a nuclear fission chain reaction is controlled to produce energy in the form of electricity

Proton – a positively charged subatomic particle found in the nucleus of an atom

Radioactive – materials containing unstable nuclei that spontaneously decay

Radioactivity – the emission of high-energy particles from the spontaneous decay of unstable nuclei

Repulsion – the equal pushing away of two materials with the same type of charge

Static electricity – electricity that is produced by friction and does not move

Thermal energy – heat energy

Decay series – shows how particular radioactive nuclei decay to produce nuclei that are stable

Nuclear fusion – the joining together of atomic nuclei producing a large amount of energy

Index

Acknowledgements

The authors and publisher would like to thank everyone who contributed images to this book:

IFC ©iStockphoto.com / Andrei Tchernov
p.15 ©iStockphoto.com / Patrick Hermans
p.26 ©iStockphoto.com / Jolande Gerritsen (desert)
p.27 ©iStockphoto.com / Carl Hagen (water lily)
p.92 ©iStockphoto.com / Debi Gardiner

ISBN 978-1-905129-75-1

Published by Lonsdale, a division of Huveaux Plc.

Authors: Aleksander Jedrosz
Susan Loxley
Ron Holt

Project Editor: Katie Smith

Editor: Rebecca Skinner

Cover and concept design: Sarah Duxbury

Designer: Anne-Marie Taylor

Artwork: HL Studios

Periodic Table

Key

Mass number →

$$\begin{array}{c} 1 \\ \textbf{H} \\ \text{hydrogen} \\ 1 \end{array}$$

Atomic number (Proton number) →

1	2											3	4	5	6	7	8 or 0
																	4 **He** helium 2
7 **Li** lithium 3	9 **Be** beryllium 4											11 **B** boron 5	12 **C** carbon 6	14 **N** nitrogen 7	16 **O** oxygen 8	19 **F** fluorine 9	20 **Ne** neon 10
23 **Na** sodium 11	24 **Mg** magnesium 12											27 **Al** aluminium 13	28 **Si** silicon 14	31 **P** phosphorus 15	32 **S** sulphur 16	35.5 **Cl** chlorine 17	40 **Ar** argon 18
39 **K** potassium 19	40 **Ca** calcium 20	45 **Sc** scandium 21	48 **Ti** titanium 22	51 **V** vanadium 23	52 **Cr** chromium 24	55 **Mn** manganese 25	56 **Fe** iron 26	59 **Co** cobalt 27	59 **Ni** nickel 28	63.5 **Cu** copper 29	65 **Zn** zinc 30	70 **Ga** gallium 31	73 **Ge** germanium 32	75 **As** arsenic 33	79 **Se** selenium 34	80 **Br** bromine 35	84 **Kr** krypton 36
85 **Rb** rubidium 37	88 **Sr** strontium 38	89 **Y** yttrium 39	91 **Zr** zirconium 40	93 **Nb** niobium 41	96 **Mo** molybdenum 42	98 **Tc** technetium 43	101 **Ru** ruthenium 44	103 **Rh** rhodium 45	106 **Pd** palladium 46	108 **Ag** silver 47	112 **Cd** cadmium 48	115 **In** indium 49	119 **Sn** tin 50	122 **Sb** antimony 51	128 **Te** tellurium 52	127 **I** iodine 53	131 **Xe** xenon 54
133 **Cs** caesium 55	137 **Ba** barium 56	139 **La** lanthanum 57	178 **Hf** hafnium 72	181 **Ta** tantalum 73	184 **W** tungsten 74	186 **Re** rhenium 75	190 **Os** osmium 76	192 **Ir** iridium 77	195 **Pt** platinum 78	197 **Au** gold 79	201 **Hg** mercury 80	204 **Tl** thallium 81	207 **Pb** lead 82	209 **Bi** bismuth 83	210 **Po** polonium 84	210 **At** astatine 85	222 **Rn** radon 86
223 **Fr** francium 87	226 **Ra** radium 88	227 **Ac** actinium 89															

140 **Ce** cerium 58	141 **Pr** praseodymium 59	144 **Nd** neodymium 60	147 **Pm** promethium 61	150 **Sm** samarium 62	152 **Eu** europium 63	157 **Gd** gadolinium 64	159 **Tb** terbium 65	162 **Dy** dysprosium 66	165 **Ho** holmium 67	167 **Er** erbium 68	169 **Tm** thulium 69	173 **Yb** ytterbium 70	175 **Lu** lutetium 71
232 **Th** thorium 90	231 **Pa** protactinium 91	238 **U** uranium 92	237 **Np** neptunium 93	242 **Pu** plutonium 94	243 **Am** americium 95	247 **Cm** curium 96	247 **Bk** berkelium 97	251 **Cf** californium 98	254 **Es** einsteinium 99	253 **Fm** fermium 100	256 **Md** mendelevium 101	254 **No** nobelium 102	257 **Lw** lawrencium 103

→ The lines of elements going across are called periods.

→ The columns of elements going down are called groups.